Knowing Jesus

KNOWING JESUS

by
T. RALPH MORTON

THE WESTMINSTER PRESS
Philadelphia

BOOK DESIGN BY DOROTHY ALDEN SMITH

Published by The Westminster Press ®
Philadelphia, Pennsylvania

PRINTED IN THE UNITED STATES OF AMERICA

232
M

Library of Congress Cataloging in Publication Data

Morton, Thomas Ralph.
   Knowing Jesus.

   Includes bibliographical references.
   1.   Jesus Christ—Knowableness.   I.   Title.
BT205.M67   232   73-16342
ISBN 0-664-24982-5

To John L. Casteel

Dear John,

This little book is for you. In a very true sense it is yours already. You suggested that I should write it. And, though I felt that you could do it very much better, you persuaded me to do it and you kept me at it—by your encouragement, by your comments and questions, by your illuminating reminiscences, and by the books you brought to my notice. Without you it would never have been started. Without you it would certainly never have been finished. Whatever it has of value owes much to you, though I accept full responsibility for the opinions and the mistakes.

So now I offer it to you, not as something new and strange, but as a token of admiration and affection and of gratitude for all that I have owed to you through many years and still owe.

Ralph

Contents

Introduction

Can we really know Jesus today? After so many centuries and so much theologizing is it possible for men now to claim that they know him?

Of course we can know something about him. Most of us do, but in the end this comes down to what others tell us about him. And to hear from other people about someone is very different from knowing him ourselves.

Undoubtedly in every age since Jesus lived, men—some men at least—have claimed to know him. They are sure that they have known him as fully as they have known anyone else. They have also assumed that there was nothing strange about their knowledge. Others could know him in the same way. They have not belonged to one type or tradition or period.

It is not surprising that the first disciples should have known Jesus, for they lived with him. But it is surprising that they should take for granted the fact that those who had never seen him should still be able to know him. John could write to such people: "We can be sure that we know him if we keep his commandments."

What about those who lived centuries later? We might think that they would be content with knowing about him, but the claim to knowing him becomes even stronger. Augustine, the great African Christian of the fourth century, claimed, "I recognized the perfect man in Christ, not merely the body of man, or the soul and the body without the mind, but the soul and the mind as well as the body." Eight hundred years later the Englishman Richard of Chichester could pray: "O merciful Redeemer, friend and brother, may I know thee more clearly . . . ," whereas four hundred years after Richard, the Frenchman Blaise Pascal could build all his thinking on knowing Jesus and could claim: "Who knows him knows the reason of all things." Did these men mean more than we mean when we say we know a friend? Undoubtedly, but they meant this at least.

It was not only the thinkers who claimed to know Jesus. When men wanted to sing a new song in a new age, it was about knowing Jesus that they sang. We have Bernard of Clairvaux in the Middle Ages singing "Jesus, thou joy of loving hearts," and the hymn writers of the eighteenth and nineteenth centuries carry on the tradition in such hymns as "How sweet the name of Jesus sounds" and "What a Friend we have in Jesus." These may seem to us today as pious songs for children or fanciful imaginings, but behind their sentimentality lies the certainty that those who wrote them and those who sang them felt that they knew Jesus.

And today thousands sing songs that are as sentimental. Popular vocalists urge, "Put your hand in the hand of the Man from Galilee!" It looks as if more people now claim to know Jesus than ever before. And not only those who talk about a "Jesus revolution"; the most radical of our theologians, while doubting everything else, are quite sure that they know Jesus.

Do all these varied people know the same Jesus? And do any of them really know him? No one can say, for no one can test the personal knowledge of another person.

Is it safe to talk in this way about knowing Jesus? The teachers of the church have tended to be suspicious of this kind of talk, and many ordinary members of the church have agreed with them. The church, indeed, bears his name. It worships in his name and it prays in his name, but it has not always regarded the knowledge of him as the one thing needful. The church has undoubtedly proclaimed Jesus and preached him and pointed to him, but what it has proclaimed has often been a doctrine about him. What it has preached has often been salvation through belief in him. What it has pointed to has often been a unique title for him. It has been hesitant to state the need of a personal knowledge of him, for such personal knowledge cannot be tested. The church has preferred to make doctrine or discipline the test of being a Christian or, at least, of being a member of the church. Doctrine can be taught and discipline can be imposed. Acceptance of a creed or attendance at a service are tests that are impersonal and objective. So acceptance of doctrine or participation in the life of the church is taken by most people, both inside and outside the church, as the sign of being a Christian. Jesus has become a name or a symbol or a doctrine. He has ceased to be someone we can know.

But can we know him?

We can well appreciate how the church has always been a bit suspicious of an individual's claim to know Jesus personally by himself. When you acknowledge the claim, you open the door to all kinds of strange, subjective ideas. You give individual experience precedence over the wisdom of the past. Personal knowledge is always a challenge to accepted opinions and a threat to established institutions, and the Jesus that some claim to know seems often to be disturbing and dangerous. He is not like the heroes and sages who have been held aloft for the admiration and emulation of the young. These— Confucius, Buddha, Plato, and others of later times— lived to be old and died full of achievements, leaving their memorials in writing or in political action. Jesus does not belong to their company. He died young, no father figure but condemned as a criminal. His memorial was the cross, a sign of punishment and death. So it is not surprising that often it is those who feel themselves the victims of the fears of the old, the timid, and the sedate who want to know Jesus and claim that they do. They are sure that he is on their side and that the future, if there is to be a future, belongs to him and to them. But do they know him?

It is no wonder that the church has been chary of these claims.

We cannot any longer avoid the question of what it means to know Jesus. This question about Jesus includes the question about themselves and about life. Men are not satisfied with the answers that they think theology is giving. They want to get down to the fundamental question of their own lives. They want to know whether there is any fundamental basis to their knowledge of other people and of themselves. They want to know what is meant by the word "God." They are content that the answer should be a mystery, for they are prepared for mystery and would be suspicious of a simple answer, but they want an answer to the question of knowing Jesus, for, if they cannot know him, they cannot expect to know other people or themselves or life.

What they are really discussing is the question of knowing, of knowing anyone, not only Jesus. It is the primary question. You cannot believe in him unless you first know him. You cannot follow him unless you first know him. You cannot believe that he is still alive unless you first know him.

And "knowing" is a very personal thing. It is a human activity, perhaps the distinguishing human activity. It is something that I do and that no one else can do for me. And knowing another person is a particular kind of knowledge, perhaps the very highest kind of human knowledge. It is doubly personal: it concerns me and the person I know. My knowledge of my wife or of a friend is my knowledge and no one else's. No one can give it to me. No one can take it from me. It is not learned from anyone. It grows of itself. And it is knowledge of a particular person, not a general knowledge of people. It does not depend only on me. It depends as much on the other. My knowledge of another person is, therefore, something unique. It carries its own authenticity and bears its own authority. It is the necessary basis of freedom, faith, and love.

When we speak of knowing Jesus, it is of this kind of knowing that we are speaking, for it is the only way in which we can know a person. Information about a person, acceptance of his teaching, or belief in his achievement—all are on a different plane.

So when we talk about the possibility of knowing Jesus, we have first to ask ourselves how we know anyone. What does knowing a person mean? We all have some experience of this. We must discuss a little more fully what this common experience means. Then we have to see whether this experience helps us to understand what we mean when we talk about knowing Jesus.

Is this how we know Jesus? If it is not, then how can we be said to know him at all? We would need to give up talking about knowing him.

But if this is how we know Jesus, then two other questions arise:

Is this all there is to knowing Jesus? Or is there something special?

If this is how we know Jesus, does it give us a glimmer of light as to what it would mean to talk about knowing God?

But first the question: Do we know him at all?

Knowing Jesus

KNOWING PEOPLE

Life is knowing people

Life is a business of knowing other people. We can, if we want, discuss human life as if it were lived by individuals in isolation. We can imagine a child abandoned by his mother and brought up by wolves and think that we are studying human life at its simplest. It is life indeed, but it is not human life. It lacks the one factor that makes the start of a human life distinctive: the absolute and long dependence of the child on his mother or mother substitute. Human life is corporate life in which a man is conscious of his fellows, depends on them, and finds the meaning of his life in knowing them.

A man's conscious life begins with getting to know his mother. It is a rudimentary knowledge but fundamental. It is the beginning of knowledge. It sets him on the way to learn whatever he will learn in life. It is the basic relationship. Out of it develops our relationship with other people. Out of it also develops our ability to think about the physical world in which we live.

Human life is life with other people in love or hate, in war or cooperation. Growth from infancy lies in the widening of the circle of people a child knows and of the things he knows about. For him it is a slow business, exciting, and sometimes frightening. For the infant the circle first widens to take in his father and the other members of his family. Knowledge grows as he learns to distinguish between them. He learns to respond to them differently. As he comes to know those upon whom he depends and to distinguish them as separate persons, he comes to know himself as a person, like them but distinct.

How do we get to know others?

We do not choose our parents or the wider family into which we are born. They are given to us. They provide for us our first knowledge of life and set the basic pattern of our personal lives. But as a child grows, he begins to make contact with neighbors and contemporaries: the children with whom he plays and their parents. He begins to construct his own world through his choice of friends. He moves out from the given world of his family, who have provided him with security and with his basic knowledge of life. He has begun to enter into a wider world in which he can choose the people he wants to know and the things he wants to do. At school and at college, in factory or office he is extending his own world by the contacts he makes. These contacts may arouse fear and withdrawal, or they may inspire sympathy and dependence. To a greater extent than perhaps we often realize we choose the people we want to know. In so doing we decide the kind of person we are going to be, for by the friends we choose we decide the direction of our lives.

Contact and interest are the first needs

How do we choose those whom we want to get to know? And how do we get to know them? How does our awareness of those upon whose understanding and affection we utterly depend in infancy grow into a free relationship with those whom we choose to make our friends?

At the simplest level two things would seem always to be needed: contact and interest. In the case of an infant, contact is the warm touch of his mother and his interest is food. Thereafter, in the business of getting to know a widening circle of people the physical contact of sight and sound and touch seems always essential. This contact convinces us that we are dealing with another living and distinctive person. But when we grow up, we make such contacts daily with many people whom we would not claim to get to know. Something more is needed to make us choose from among them those whom we want to know. There has to be some spring of interest to awaken the desire to know better someone with whom we have made contact. In our youth, when curiosity is most active, is the time when we want to know all sorts of people or, at least, to know about them. We welcome contact with them, but only when interest is aroused do we get to know them. Admiration, curiosity, or even suspicion is needed to move us from simple contact to desire for more personal knowledge.

Similarity and difference are also needed

Contact and interest are only the first steps in getting to know someone. Something more is needed before we can venture to say that we know him. We need a touch of sympathy and of mystery.

We must feel that the person we have met has something fundamentally in common with us. On a first meeting this can be expressed in quite superficial ways. We are delighted when we learn that we share the same birthplace, or have been at the same school or college, or have visited the same places on holiday, or work at the same kind of job, or have a mutual friend. This happy acceptance of a trivial connection indicates our hope of finding something in common at a deeper level. This may be a common interest in work or politics or sport. It may be something far less tangible but more abiding. It may be some common attitude that transcends very different opinions.

It is often difficult to see what two close friends have in common. It need not be shared politics or a common religion or a similar job or like artistic tastes. Samuel Johnson and James Boswell must have known each other as well as two men ever have, yet they were very different in age, in social background, in character, and in many of their interests. The only thing of which we can be sure is that they did know each other well. What they shared was a common humanity. Each recognized it in the other in a quite special way. This sense of having something fundamental in common is essential and the first step in getting to know someone well. It is so obvious that it may sound silly to mention it, but we do not take it for granted in the people we chance to meet. We look anxiously for something in common. Our fear of not finding it is seen in our use of the word "stranger." He is one who is not like us.

It is difficult to determine what two friends have in common beyond their humanity. The reason is that also necessary is the surprise of finding that the other person is different from oneself and from everyone else. He is in some way unpredictable and mysterious. This sense of the unexpected is what attracts us in a new acquaintance as much as the comfortable assurance of his being of the same stuff as oneself.

It is this combination of the familiar and the mysterious that makes friendship an inexplicable thing and the nature of "knowing" difficult to define. A man can never be certain that two of his close friends will take to each other. He may well encounter a certain antipathy between them. One reason for this is that the business of getting to know someone is always a two-way affair. We may think that we alone choose our friends. We forget that they must also choose us. We can, therefore, never pass our friends on to others and expect them to be adopted without question. In getting to know someone, we cease to be a sole determining agent. We have become both subject and object. In other words, we have entered the free world of other people.

The risk of knowing others

Most of us are lucky enough at one time or another to have entered into an exciting new relationship with someone. When we did so, we found that life had acquired a new dimension of interest and understanding. We may even have found ourselves traveling in a new and unexpected direction. When we get to know someone, we can never tell where this new knowledge will lead us or how much we will be changed in the process. Our joy in life depends on our ability to enter freely into new relationships. Our response to this wider society often depends on the attitude to other people that we have learned in our close and given family circle and on the kind of society that surrounds us. This business of getting to know people is a very personal activity, rewarding in its consequences but dangerous.

Awareness of this danger often makes parents anxious about the friends their children make. Parents may even feel that they should be allowed to choose their children's friends. And society can be very suspicious of any close friendship outside marriage. Today in particular we tend to feel that there is something unhealthy in the close friendship of two men or two women. In the eyes of many it is safer not to know other people too intimately, to keep oneself to oneself. And so we erect all kinds of subtle barriers against people's getting to know one another.

And yet loneliness is one of the things that we dread most. It is certainly one of the most acute forms of suffering. As George Macdonald said, the sense of being my own is the one principle of hell. Loneliness is the bitter-est taste of hell that many people know. Most of us are aware that if we are to live, we must have someone near us whom we know and who knows us. We know that, despite all its dangers and demands, friendship is the key to life, to its meaning, and to its joy.

"The only real thing in the world"

Most people know that friendship is the key to life, but it is not only ordinary people who know this. It has also been the teaching of the philosophers. In Scotland the Gifford lecturers have long been regarded as among the most respected of teachers. They are not likely to be either young or rash. They might be a bit wordy, but then they have to deliver two long courses of lectures. They tend to be a bit ponderous, but they know that few will be there to listen to them. They consider carefully and choose their words well.

One of the liveliest, John MacMurray, in the introduc-tion to his Gifford lectures, wrote: "All meaningful knowledge is for the sake of action, and all meaningful action for the sake of friendship." [1]

An earlier Gifford lecturer, A. E. Taylor, went so far as to find in friendship a clue to the meaning of eternal life. "At a higher level than that of mere animal enjoy-ment, such as we may get from basking before a good fire, or giving ourselves to the delight of a hot bath, we know how curiously the consciousness of past and future falls away when we are, for example, spending an eve-ning of prolonged enjoyment in the company of wholly

congenial friends. . . . If we are truly enjoying ourselves, the time passed, as we say, 'like anything.' I have
heard that the late R. L. Nettleship was in the habit of
dwelling on this expression as indicating the real meaning of eternity." [2] Many of us have, surely, been fortunate
enough to have had a momentary taste of this experience.

On a very different line J. M. E. McTaggart, the Cam-
bridge psychologist, wrote in a letter to a friend: "But
it can't be nice to believe in God, I should think. It
would be horrible to think that there was anyone who
was closer to one than one's friends. I want to feel, and
I do feel, that my love for them and the same love that
other people have for their friends is the only real thing
in the world." [3] Most of us would agree that the love of
our friends is a very real thing and that it leads us into a
deeper understanding of the love that other people have
for theirs. But we would doubt his conclusion that it
makes the idea of God repulsive. For many it is what
makes it possible.

The search for an authentic person

These statements by respectable philosophers of an
earlier generation emphasize the satisfaction and joy
they themselves found in knowing other men and women
and the clue that this has provided their understanding of the meaning of life. To many young people today
they will probably sound very fortunate and a bit com-
placent. They know that the comfortable, sheltered, lei-
surely life of the academic philosopher is not for them.
The world that awaits them offers fewer attractions, and

indeed only, in the words of Peter Marin, "a kind of grimness and weariness, a kind of loneliness." [4] But in their often strident revolt against the morals and conventions of their elders they are trying, perhaps not very successfully, to assert their right to a life of their own, in which they can find something of eternal significance. And perhaps those who take to themselves the name of Jesus are showing that they are aware that life is a matter of knowing someone. Dr. Carl Rogers has said that what the patient in psychotherapy is seeking is "a meeting with an authentic person." It is not only patients who are on this quest. Many others would not claim to have found what they are looking for. But they know that it is to be found with other people, in the hope of finding someone who is authentic.

Those who met Jesus came to know him in the same way

The immediate impact that Jesus made upon those who met him in Palestine was undoubtedly that they were meeting an authentic person. The stories of his meeting with people constitute the irreducible minimum of the Gospel records. The four Gospels give us the only facts we have about the life of Jesus. But their purpose was not to write his biography in the modern manner—a study of his life and times with all references quoted. In fact, they constitute our references beyond which we cannot go. Their purpose was different: they were written to record the impression that Jesus had made on his first disciples and to indicate the faith to which their meeting with him had led them. More particularly, they were written for use in the churches as material for worship and teaching. They were concerned with getting over to men ideas that were novel and startling. They reflected, as every book must, the opinions and prejudices of their authors. They reflected also the needs of the particular group for which each was written. Each Gospel, therefore, expressed a particular point of view and served a particular interest. We may regard them as colored by the personal experiences and opinions of the author and distorted by the propaganda needs of a particular group. We may doubt the accuracy of some of the reporting and suspect its interpretation. But, however critical we are, we are left with the basic accounts of Jesus' meeting with people.

The thread that holds together the various incidents and teachings of the Gospels is Jesus' meeting with all sorts of people: the needy and the fortunate, the pompous and the pious, men, women and children, officials, merchants, priests, soldiers, teachers, prostitutes, madmen. They interrupt what he is doing and claim the right to accost him. After we have questioned everything about the Gospels, this is what remains. Men could have added—and did—didactic comment. They could have distorted—and undoubtedly did distort—the stories he told. They could have failed to understand the things he did, and later they confessed as much. But no one could have invented these meetings or would have wanted to do so. If they had tried to do so, the artificiality of their attempts would soon have been apparent.

One incident may be taken as an example. It is fully

told in Luke's Gospel and is, indeed, central to the story as Luke tells it.

"One of the Pharisees invited him to eat with him; he went to the Pharisee's house and took his place at table. A woman who was living an immoral life in the town had learned that Jesus was at table in the Pharisee's house and had brought oil of myrrh in a small flask. She took her place behind him, by his feet, weeping. His feet were wetted with her tears and she wiped them with her hair, kissing them and anointing them with the myrrh. When his host the Pharisee saw this he said to himself, 'If this fellow were a real prophet, he would know who this woman is that touches him, and what sort of woman she is, a sinner.' Jesus took him up and said, 'Simon, I have something to say to you.' 'Speak on, Master,' said he. 'Two men were in debt to a money-lender: one owed him five hundred silver pieces, the other fifty. As neither had anything to pay with he let them both off. Now, which will love him most?' Simon replied, 'I should think the one that was let off most.' 'You are right,' said Jesus. Then turning to the woman, he said to Simon, 'You see this woman? I came to your house: you provided no water for my feet; but this woman has made my feet wet with her tears and wiped them with her hair. You gave me no kiss; but she has been kissing my feet ever since I came in. You did not anoint my head with oil; but she has anointed my feet with myrrh. And so, I tell you, her great love proves that her many sins have been forgiven; where little has been forgiven, little love is shown.' Then he said to her, 'Your sins are forgiven.' The other guests began to ask themselves, 'Who is this, that he can forgive sins?' But he said to the woman, 'Your faith has saved you; go in peace.' " (Luke 7:36–50, NEB.)

We can see how the record of this incident was used to point the difficult lesson of forgiveness and to expose Phariseeism inside the church. But the story goes far beyond this in dramatic detail and in the portrayal of character—the host's condescension and his feeling of generosity in entertaining this odd prophet, the embarrassing situation in which the woman put them all, Jesus' desire to save her face and his willingness to rebuke his host, and then the irritation of his fellow guests.

This incident, so fully recorded, is only one of many. Among those who met him, there was a surprising variety. They were generally not the important or the privileged. Many of them were women. In their meeting the initiative generally came from them and not from him, but it was always a mutual encounter. Jesus responded to them and they responded further to him.

Contact and interest; similarity and difference

These meetings of men and women with Jesus follow the pattern by which in ordinary life we come to know our friends. First, there was the point of contact. Then there was the awakening of interest, followed by the realization that here was a man made of the same stuff as they were and, lastly, the conviction that he was in his own strange way quite different.

Contact was obvious. It was contact at its very simplest—the contact of sight and speech and touch. It took place where men ordinarily met—on the road, by the lake, in people's houses. And the interest he aroused was also obvious: the interest of curiosity or need or suspicion. But as strong as the interest and as simple as the contact was the unquestioning conviction that he was one of themselves. He had been born among them, brought up with them, worked among them as a carpenter. He was known to them from infancy. He was related to some of them. He was no stranger, not even a well-intentioned, superior visitor from Jerusalem. He enjoyed no privilege of education, wealth, or position. The one disability under which he suffered was that he was the carpenter's son: "Can . . . any good thing come out of Nazareth?" This sense of his belonging to them and of their belonging to him shines through the records. No one, least of all children or women, the unpopular or the unfortunate, showed any hesitation in approaching him. Each felt that they knew him and that he knew them. He was one of them by birth, by daily life, and simply by being a man.

This sense of common humanity made it easy for people to meet him, but it also marked him off from everyone else. It was this unique commonness which made men want to meet him, but it was in his unique commonness that he was different from others. Most of us don't want to be common in the sense of being no different from other people. We want to have something about us that is easily recognized as special and unique, but Jesus seemed never to make any claim for himself that he did not make for everyone else. He said that others could do what he did. He was not the great man who lorded it over them. He was not like their leaders who claimed to be benefactors. He was not like their teachers who ex-

alted in their position and their education as signs of
their authority. He seemed to make no pretensions apart
from that of being a man. He let the needs of others dic-
tate his daily actions. He was closest to those who had
no place in society. He did not avoid men's opposition
and he died as a criminal.

This attitude of being one with them was expressed
in his teaching. It was not difficult to understand, but
it was difficult to accept. And it was dangerous. In the
eyes of many it was blasphemous. Essentially his blas-
phemy lay in the common claim he made for all men.
He saw men as called to a willing acceptance of all
other men and therefore to a love of them. He was no
sentimentalist. He did not expect men not to suffer. He
knew the world's cruelty and its unanswered questions.
He saw the world differently from other men, because
he saw it as it was, as God's world. In the same way, he
accepted all men as the sons of God. He was not angry
at the world but only with those who despised any part
of it. His teaching, to the surprise of men, was about
happiness. We treat his Beatitudes as religious platitudes.
He was asserting the strange and unacceptable luck of
the poor, the hungry, and the meek. This was his glad
acceptance of himself as a common man, one with all
other men. He did not identify himself with them. He
was one of them. This was unique and very strange.

Those who met Jesus would never have claimed that
they knew all about him. There was plenty about him
that they could not understand and plenty that they
could not accept—plenty to mystify them, many questions still unanswered. In other words, they knew him as

we know our friends. They enjoyed meeting him and wanted to go on knowing him.

The risk of knowing him

Their knowing him, even in this casual way, always meant a change in their lives. Some few knew that they must go with him even though they did not like the way he took. Others went away because they felt that he demanded too much of them, but even they were never quite the same again. They were left with new uncertainties and new self-questionings. For some it meant healing and a difficult return to ordinary life. For some it meant acute suffering, as Mary, his mother, found. For Judas it meant suicide. For most of the disciples it meant a life they could not have foreseen or desired. For Pilate and Caiaphas, responsible for his death, their encounter with Jesus may have been just one of those incidents in their official lives which they were glad to forget, or it may have remained a haunting memory. It would depend on whether they had in any real sense encountered him as a person, as he had encountered them, or whether they had managed to treat him merely as another case. All those who had in any way come to know him found that their lives had attained a new dimension and taken a new direction. In this the effect of knowing Jesus was not different from the effect that coming to know someone has on us. If we want to make comparisons, we could say that the effect seems to have been more certain, wider in its range, and more unpredictable in its results. But there would be no essential difference in kind.

It never occurred to them to describe or diagnose the effect that knowing Jesus had on them, even as it does not occur to us to diagnose our response to our friends or theirs to us. We find their company always pleasant and sometimes exciting. We want to go on enjoying it. Those who got to know Jesus in Palestine were probably much the same. He had brought new joy into their lives, all kinds of questions about the future, and, above all, a new freedom. In all the recorded incidents of his meeting with men and women we find this new note of liberty, either in actuality or in hope. It may have been freedom from disease or freedom from fear. It may have been liberation from convention and the niggling demands of the law. Often it was a new and embarrassing freedom in their relation with those whom they had previously avoided. Sometimes it meant a new freedom of action in their domestic lives. Sometimes it spoke of freedom to hope in an impossible world, but always there was the gift of freedom in some form. It was terrifying for those whose lives depended on the security of the familiar and who were not prepared to live life at any risk. But they could not fail to recognize the reality of this freedom, for they saw it explicit in Jesus himself. It was the basis of that friendliness which Martin Luther saw in Jesus and which he declared to be the one thing we had to know if we were to know God.[5]

The Jesus men knew

The picture of Jesus that we get from the Gospels is not the picture that men drew when they became more interested in doctrine than in experience. Then the picture was drawn to support a theory. Nor was this the picture that men painted on the walls of their churches when more than two centuries later they were allowed to have buildings of their own for worship. Then it was the triumph of the faith that they wanted to record. But this human picture is the one that down the centuries men have rediscovered, hidden in dim memories and in the accounts of those who knew him in the flesh. It is the picture that persists in men's experience presumably because it is based on the social memory of the truth. That part of the Gospel record which is untouched by doctrine and almost uncolored by moralistic application is that which records Jesus' meeting with men, women, and children.

Indeed, at one level, below that of textual and doctrinal questions, the four Gospels can be taken as some of the most valuable and concise material we have for studying how we get to know people. This was not the reason for their being written, but the fact that the meetings recorded are incidental and often accidental makes them the more reliable and the more valuable. The men and women who met Jesus would have echoed the words of the philosophers already quoted. Certainly they found in knowing Jesus "the only real thing in the world," so that when he was killed their life was in ruins. And equally certainly some found in knowing him the meaning of eternal life.

These men and women knew Jesus with all the immediacy of physical contact, and with physical contact they did not need to ask for more. Without this elementary, physical contact there can be no communication between men, no speech, no mutual knowledge. As John MacMurray wrote: "We communicate with each other only through our bodies; by acting in the world." [6]

This is the way in which Jesus communicated with men. It is the only way in which we can communicate with one another. In meeting him men met a particular man, born in a particular place at a particular time and given a particular name—Jesus—by his father. We lose our way in a labyrinth of speculation unless we are continually brought back to this basic fact.

In the end we know about Jesus today only because some men and women had bodily contact with him hundreds of years ago. We would not know anything about him if they had not known him in this personal, physical way. We should not be offended by this elementary fact. All our knowledge is founded on its general truth. The knowledge of the world that each one of us has acquired and without which we could not live is based on the elementary knowledge that each one of us learned in infancy from his mother. Basic knowledge is not knowing about things or knowing that things happen or even knowing about people; it is just knowing people. This is the knowledge on which all our other knowledge is built. This is how I learn to know: by learning to know other people, and so myself, and, through others, the world. I learn through what

Martin Buber calls the process of "distance and relation." [7] I learn to know that I am a person distinct from others and yet that my life can be found only in relation to them.

What is certain is that any knowledge we have of Jesus, however simple or profound, goes back to this ordinary knowledge that some men and women had of Jesus as a friend. All that has followed is built on this. The beginning of the church, the spread of the faith, worship, doctrine, and theology—all rest on this personal, human knowledge that men had of Jesus.

We today can never know him in this immediate, personal, intimate, physical way.

But if we cannot know him in this way firsthand, can we be said to know him at all?

Can we with honesty talk today about knowing Jesus?

CHAPTER

2

KNOWING ABOUT PEOPLE

Is face-to-face meeting the only way of knowing people?

We take it for granted that personal, physical contact is essential if we want to know someone. We are so sure that there is no substitute for the briefest face-to-face encounter that we go to absurd lengths just to be able to say that we have seen or heard or spoken to or even shaken hands with someone in the news. We feel that this gives us some claim to know him. And there may be something in it. The briefest of personal contacts may give us a chance for personal assessment that we cannot get through television, radio, or the press. We feel that firsthand contact is better than secondhand reporting even though we know that meeting people can be as impersonal as collecting autographs.

This attitude is as old as the New Testament. In the Fourth Gospel we read how certain Greeks wanted to see Jesus. They did not give any particular reason. They did not plead a need for healing. They did not express the desire to ask a question. Apparently they wanted only to be able to say that they had met this man Jesus. At least Jesus was not particularly interested in their desire to see him. There is no further mention of them. Instead, Jesus goes on to speak of his approaching death, as he often did when the outside world forced itself on his attention. He seemed not to feel that just for them to have a word with him would achieve anything. If they were ever to know him, it would be only after his death.

We sometimes talk as if it would make all the difference to us if we had had the chance of meeting Jesus in the flesh, even if only for a few seconds. We feel that we live in an unsatisfactory world of remote reporting. How can we claim to know someone we have never met? But would a brief meeting have necessarily meant so much to us? There is a great deal more to knowing a person than just meeting him for a moment. Most of us meet a great many people of whose existence we are soon quite unaware. And there are plenty of people whom we have never met who are far more real to us than many of our chance acquaintances. Our understanding of the world and our enjoyment of it would be very limited if the only people we knew about were those with whom we have physical contact. If our experience of the world were confined to personal contact, at its most superficial, and secondhand reporting, we would end up by seeing only ourselves and time and the world as ours.

Our unaccountable debt to those whom we have never seen

We call it our world because it is the only world we know, but it is certainly not of our making. It has been made for us by those whom we have never seen. Its present form is due to an innumerable multitude of men and women in the past, and our way of dealing with it and of thinking about it is particularly due to what we have learned from them. We know a lot quite intimately about some of them—our immediate ancestors, and those who have set the pattern of our family life, and our national leaders who have set the pattern of our social and national life. We have heard of many more. Some are very dim figures. Others are so dominant in our social memory that we think we know a lot about them. This endless succession of those whom we have never seen has had as great an influence upon our lives as the small circle of intimate acquaintances who share our personal life today. The latter determine the style of our life in the little bit of the world we call our own. The former have drawn the pattern of the greater world that surrounds us.

We are alive today because other men lived yesterday and all the previous yesterdays. Men have always been aware that the life into which they have been born is a continuing life. This awareness of continuity is one of the things that distinguish human life from other forms of life. It has given men a sense of history and the uncomfortable knowledge that everything familiar is liable to change. In most of the human race it is expressed in some form of ancestor worship, which links a man personally to the past and enables him to look to the future. Today, when we are so conscious of discontinuity and the extreme rapidity of change, we cling more than ever before to the reminders of our past. We treasure the diaries and letters and all the relics of our predecessors. In this we show how much we feel that we need to know our ancestors if we are to understand our position in the world today.

We want to know more about them

We want to choose those whom we will know most about. We don't want our knowledge of the past to be limited to "our fathers that begat us" or to the heroes offered to us in our youth—"famous men . . . such as did bear rule in their kingdoms, . . . men renowned for their power, . . . leaders of the people by their counsels, . . . such as sought out musical tunes and set forth verses in writing." Just as we need to break out of our families to make our own friends, so we want to escape from the tyranny of our traditions to find heroes of our own choosing. Perhaps, to continue the quotation, we want to be reminded that "some there be which have no memorial; who are perished as though they had not been." Our life is just as much built on the meek who through disasters and wars have cultivated the soil and cared for their children as on the renowned leaders of the people, only we do not know so much about them. It is up to us to choose whom we will know about and who will act as signposts for the direction of our lives.

The choice of our friends from the past can be as important for the direction of our lives as the choice of our living companions. It can also be as much a matter of chance, of locality, interest, or protest. A man cannot work in a particular place without developing an interest in those who worked there before him. We are interested in those whose discoveries have changed our lives but whose experiences we can never share. We want to know what it was like to do something for the first time—to discover America or to walk on the moon. Or we may want to learn from the rebels, the revolutionaries in thought and action who have changed or attempted to change the world's history. Or we may be fascinated by those whose grandiose ambitions came to nothing, whose failures have affected our lives more than other people's successes—Napoleon or Hitler. Or we may feel that the men who have given meaning to life have been the philosophers, the artists, the saints, and the sages. We may want to learn something from them. Life would be the poorer and the world much less comprehensible if the source of our knowledge were limited to the small circle in which most of us live our lives. Our national life, our local social life, all art and science, and, of course, the life of the church depend on the nature of the experiences passed down by millions whom we have never known and by a few of whom we know a little.

We have to work for our knowledge of our friends of the past

The choice of whom we want to know is up to us, and so is the job of getting to know them. For most of us the selection is casual and haphazard and our attention to them offhand, but there have been those who have assiduously and happily cultivated their friends distant in time. The historian Macaulay saw the people of seventeenth-century England and the men and women of both ancient Greece and the Roman Empire as familiar acquaintances whom he knew intimately. They were as well known to him as his much loved contemporaries in early nineteenth-century England. He treated the books they had written and the books others had written about them as his means of conversing with them. The volumes in his library were full of his written comments and questions, as if in his reading he were continually discussing events with them and putting his questions to them. He did not read books just to gather information or to pass an examination or to write another book but because he wanted to understand those of the past. He wanted to get to know them. And he claimed that he did, but it was an unending process.

The fact that he treated the characters in Greek drama and in the plays of Shakespeare in the same way might suggest that their historical existence did not matter at all. But there are two points here: The first is that in trying to get to know a historical or fictional character we are really trying to understand ourselves. Most of us would admit that Hamlet is nearer to us as a person than William the Conqueror and that Romeo and Juliet are a more understandable couple than William and Mary. We're interested in them because we're interested in ourselves. By seeing them in situations quite foreign to us we begin to understand ourselves better. This first point applies also to historical characters. But with them is a second and very important point: What they did has affected us. We want to understand their situation so that we can understand our own better. They help us to see how we got into the position we are in. We are trying to find in our knowledge of them a clue to our present life and its problems. We bring our present situation into our understanding of them. This is why there can never be a final, definitive biography of any hero or villain of the past. Each age has to interpret the men of the past afresh. Its problems are different and, therefore, its questions are different. So each age rewrites the history of the past and the lives of its heroes. It is because they are historical people that we read and write their lives. We have to know them to know ourselves.

The picture we have of our present world depends to a great extent on the kind of people in the past whom we have chosen to get to know and the lessons they have taught us. It is often through their examples that we find our place in the world and educate ourselves to act in it. The people whom we admire and seek to understand affect us profoundly. As William James wrote: "It is a fundamental truth that we become like what we attend to with complete seriousness." Most of us can probably think of someone who consciously modeled himself on someone he reverences: a politician on another politician, an artist on his master, a student on his teacher. Sometimes there is a touch of pedantry in it and we are amused, but more often there has been real inspiration and flowering of understanding. And the model may well belong to the past.

Carl Sandburg, in writing his massive six-volume life of Abraham Lincoln, became so identified with Lincoln that in his later years he came to be regarded as a second Lincoln. He had never met Lincoln. He had never seen him. He, indeed, shared with Lincoln the same prairie background of Indiana and Illinois. He so steeped himself in every intimate detail not only of Lincoln but also of every other person and every place and house involved in his life, that as you read the book, you find it hard to decide who is speaking—Lincoln or Sandburg. Not that it seems to matter. Sandburg is so identified with Lincoln that the reader finds he too is identified with Lincoln in understanding, sympathy, and humor.

This was an identification expressed in the writing of an immense and detailed biography. It is more usual to see the identification with the admired hero expressed in action. William Dean Howells, American novelist of the last century, wrote of Tolstoi as "precisely the human being with whom at the moment I find myself in the greatest intimacy; not because I know him, but because I know myself through him." This coming to understand oneself better is, of course, part of the process of identification. With Howells, as with many another, it meant also a changed direction in his life.

He found his political views changing in line with Tolstoi's.

There is in this nothing exciting like the immediate appeal of a charismatic contemporary, but, because getting to know someone in the past demands application and study, our understanding may be deeper and more lasting in its effects. We have to rely on our own interest, our own efforts, and our own intelligence. We have to apply his actions and his thoughts to our own situation. We have all the work to do. He does nothing, but what we learn is our own.

They teach us by their death

There is another and very important respect in which our knowledge of our friends in the past differs from our knowledge of our contemporary and living friends. For our living friends, as for ourselves, the future is unknown. We do not know what will happen to them or what they will do. The mystery of the unknown shrouds the future. With our friends in the past, there is no uncertain future. We know, or can know, the whole of their lives up to the very end. We know their final catastrophe or achievement, their final failure or success. (We know that Abraham Lincoln was assassinated.) We can assess their lives and achievements in their fullness. We can penetrate to the inner meaning of their lives without trying to describe them in terms of triumph or defeat, satisfaction or disappointment. Perhaps something like this was in Jesus' mind when he did not see the Greeks but talked instead of his own death. Men from outside his immediate circle would be able to see him only when he was dead, for only so would they see him whole. There is obvious truth in this. On a much humbler plane but in the same way, a man often comes to know his father fully after he has died. A child is too near his parents and too dependent on them to know them fully as persons. Even when the son has grown up, there are facts in his father's life and sides to his character that he does not know anything about until the father has died. Then he often finds from old letters, diaries, and the memories of contemporaries things of which he had no idea while his father was living. The separation of death brings knowledge. We see the finished life, and we see the life in its fullness. This is something that our living friends can never teach us.

This knowledge of death is one of the greatest gifts that our past friends make to our knowledge of life. We know that they have died. It is the one fact common to them all. We know that we shall die, but we know that without their lives and their deaths there would have been no life for us in the world today. We know that life goes on and that it is precariously in our hands. Without them we could not have learned this wisdom.

Knowing about Jesus

We know about Jesus in the same way that we know about other people in the past. The trouble is that more people have known more about him than about anyone else. Whether more people in the world today know more about him than about Buddha or Confucius or

Napoleon or Marx would be impossible to calculate, but at least in the West some knowledge of Jesus is so woven into tradition, art, literature, law, government, not to mention the church, that it would be almost impossible to find someone to whom the name of Jesus meant nothing at all. Even the ejaculation "Jesus Christ" indicates some acquaintance.

Because of this a mystery always hangs over this inevitable knowledge of Jesus. It is due partly to the variety of ways in which he is presented to men. It is perhaps due even more to uncertainty of the kind of person he was: proclaimed a victor, yet the representative of the poor and the meek and the suffering; his memorial a cross, not a literary masterpiece or a new nation or even a defeated cause; put to death as a young man, yet passionately regarded as alive. It is no wonder that different people know so many different things about him, nor is it any wonder that there are those who claim that we cannot now really know anything about him at all.

But, in the end, we know about him, as we know about anyone else, through other people: through what his contemporaries reported of him, through what as children we were taught about him and (as important) what we overheard our elders say about him, and through what others in the past have thought about him. Such knowledge begins to have meaning, as any knowledge begins to have meaning, only as we are confronted by the tensions of our own life and begin to ask questions of the meaning of life and death.

We can get to know about him only if we want to

and if we do some work. Knowledge about a person or about a thing does not come to us unsought, however much we may be bombarded by other people's knowledge.

We know about Jesus first from gossip

As children we overhear his name in sanctimonious or flippant tones. We see his supposed picture in classroom, church, or shop and are not attracted. If we are lucky, we realize that he is someone whom some adults take seriously. We may get some formal teaching about him, but even if we don't, we learn something about him because his name is involved in so much that we learn at school. We can't get away from what men have written and we have read, from what men say and we hear, from all the varied and distorted rumors and gossip and reasoned opinions of present acquaintances and past generations, and from the knowledge of the strange things that men and women have believed and done in his name. The written records about him are always at hand—in schools and shops, in hotel bedrooms, and on our bookshelves. Of no other person of the past can this be said. But as far as most of us are concerned, it is all gossip about him.

We know him from the records

We have to choose to know him. We have to want to get to know about him. We don't know about him just because he is so much a part of our world that we never need to explain who he is when his name is mentioned. We may know very little about him even though his name is so easily on people's lips as an oath or a symbol or a hope. Getting to know anyone is something we have to do for ourselves. And sometimes even with a contemporary we have to surmount a barrier of reluctance that we have built up against the gossip of our friends and their special pleading. Something may have to happen to make us want to know him. In the same way we can, and many of us do in youth, put off wanting to know Jesus because of the talk we have heard about him and the crude desire of some that we ought to get to know about him. This is a far greater obstacle for many than any difficulty in reading the records.

When we ourselves turn to the records written about Jesus—the Gospels—there are inevitable questions of reliability and interpretation, as there are for any book that we read. And they are the same questions: What does this mean? Is it true? Do I believe it? Has it any significance now for me? As with any old book there are questions of text, and as with any book at all there are questions of interpretation, but we can easily be bogged down in matters of text and interpretation as if by the finding of the original text all our difficulties would be at an end. The questions would remain because they are our questions. Indeed, we should be glad that there is no foolproof text and no guaranteed explanation of the meaning of all the words. It is not the textual critic or the lecturer who knows Shakespeare best but the actor who has to make the words his own and act them out on the stage. Imagination and action are as much needed for interpretation as scholarship.

We read the Gospels to know about Jesus, not to study the text. This is the purpose for which they were written, as Shakespeare's plays were written—to be acted, not to be studied.

What we should be doing when we read the Gospels is to ask questions and express our doubts and disagreements. We should do with the Gospels what Macaulay did with his books—not just underline the phrases that appeal to us but add our question marks and our opinions. It is never an easy business to get to know someone in the past. It was not an easy business for Sandburg to get to know all about Abraham Lincoln, though he was a fellow countryman separated by only a generation. It involved the work of a lifetime. In the case of Jesus it is infinitely harder. We know about his life only through the words of men who spoke a different language and had a very different background from ours. We can get to know him with personal knowledge only if we want to know about him as keenly as Sandburg wanted to know about Lincoln. And we can do so only if we have a deep concern about the situation we and other men are in today. We must come with our experience of love, suffering, and hope. And, above all, we must come with our unanswered questions. It is only in such a spirit that we shall get anything out of a book. In the Gospels we learn about Jesus through the minds and memories of those who knew him personally. We learn to know about Jesus by learning to know about them also.

We know about Jesus through others in the past

George Fox, the founder of the Society of Friends in England in the seventeenth century, said of Jesus: "There is one, even Jesus Christ, that can speak to my condition." He explained his condition as that of being tempted by the devil. He saw Jesus as tempted by the same devil. This was the particular view of one particular man. We have no reason to doubt that this was how he saw Jesus. Men have varied widely in the ways by which they have described Jesus. They have given him many titles and seen him as fulfilling many roles. Their particular experiences have defied generalization in abstract terms. So theology, which must use general terms, has been chary of particular experience. The church has seen the acceptance of doctrine about Jesus as more important than knowing him or even knowing about him.

But this should not blind us to the fact that there has always been hidden in its life and expressed in its worship a sustaining knowledge of Jesus, which sometimes seems withered but at other times breaks into life. At these times men seem to feel that they must get to know something for themselves about him. Something uncomfortable in their condition or in the condition of society seems to be needed to awaken this desire. For George Fox it was the horror of being subject to temptations that he could not resist; for others in other conditions the impulse was different. But it has arisen from dissatisfaction with the conditions of their lives and a desire to find a better way for themselves and others. Their search and their findings down the centuries have assisted greatly in our knowing about Jesus today. They have helped to bridge the passage of the years between his day and ours.

It would manifestly be impossible to give even a summary sketch of the men and women who down the ages have claimed to know Jesus and in so doing have added to our knowledge about him. It would as clearly be an impertinence to assess the nature of their knowledge. All that can be done is to mention some of the more significant periods during which men have spoken about Jesus in a particular way. By their words they have added to our knowledge of him. We can never stand with the first disciples—we cannot ever share their physical contact with Jesus in the flesh—but we do stand with all those who have come to know about him since. Whatever their questions, whatever the tensions of their lives, they are not strange to us.

Through Paul and his friends

Paul and his friends had just missed seeing Jesus. For them the one certain fact was that he had been put to death on the cross. If they were to know him, they had to accept his death and face what it meant for themselves and for the world. The death of Jesus was always in the forefront of Paul's thinking. The thought of such a man ending his life as a criminal—a scandal to the Jews and foolishness to the Greeks—was something that he could not banish from his mind. He had to make it the center of his living and his thinking. "I determined not to know any thing among you, save Jesus Christ, and him crucified." (I Cor. 2:2.) So he wrote to the church at Corinth. He knew that life could have no meaning and men could have no hope unless they could know Jesus as ever living in this world. This was not a theory he had to accept but a person he had to know. To know Jesus was his aim and his desire: "That I may know him, and the power of his resurrection, and the fellowship of his sufferings" (Phil. 3:10). In the process he was coming to know himself and other men in a new light. In the light of Jesus he was being brought into a corporate knowledge that included all other men. He was waiting to know fully, but at the same time he was aware that the knowledge was already there all about him. "Now I know in part; but then shall I know even as also I am known." (I Cor. 13:12.) He saw not only himself but the whole world as finding its meaning and its glory in Jesus. He had emerged into the liberty of hope for all men. In this faith he went out, not to claim a hostile world for Jesus, but to acclaim all men as belonging to this newly sighted world, the only real world, God's world.

Paul and the group he represented are of cardinal importance to us still. They had not known Jesus in the flesh, but they were sure that they had to get to know him and could. They were aware of acute political and social tensions in the Roman world of their time, and these were paralleled by personal tension in their own lives. It was this which made Paul desperate to know Jesus. Inevitably the words in which Paul tried to explain his experience in terms that the men of his time could understand have received more attention because of their difficulty than the experience of knowing Jesus, which was the cause of his writing, but which cannot easily be expressed in words. We always have to be reminded of the fact that the spring of all Paul's thoughts and actions was the determination to know Jesus.

Through those who found him in love and joy

It has not been in the ongoing conventions of church life that a new impulse to get to know Jesus has usually appeared. Rather, it has been among the unconventional, the dissatisfied, the rebellious, the odd groups, or even among the divergent, the heretical, the seeking. But sometimes they were different. In the later Middle Ages men came to know a gentler Jesus—the child Jesus. Their quest was in response to changes in society and the demands of new questions. Life had lost much of the grimness and terror of the Dark Ages. Commerce and the manor had taken over from war and the castle. Towns and civic life were developing. A quite new pattern of domestic life was emerging. Family letters took the place of monkish chronicles. Schools and universities came into existence. How were Christians to react to these unheroic conditions? How were they to see Jesus in the very different tensions of a more pacific life? We know how Francis of Assisi reacted—by abandoning his family affluence and embracing the poverty of Jesus. For the sake of the poor and the suffering he was protesting against the power and the comfort of the rich. Because he saw the beauty of all material things and had sympathy for every living creature he protested against the blind-ness and the cruelty of men. And in all that he was doing he felt he was following Jesus' example, for this was how he knew Jesus.

The articulate saints were giving to people a new picture of the human Jesus, easier for them to recognize. As William James wrote: "Christian saints have had their specialities of devotion, Saint Francis to Christ's wounds; Saint Anthony of Padua to Christ's childhood; Saint Bernard to his humanity." [8] This human figure was por-trayed in popular art, in song, and in drama and so be-came widely familiar to people, alongside and sometimes taking the place of the figure on the crucifix. "What shines out from the medieval carol, and from other medieval religious lyrics, is the intense poetry of the subject matter, the extreme expressiveness of the story of Christ's life and death as a revelation of the nature of God." [9] Many of these could best be described as love poems, with Jesus not as the beloved but as the lover. They are in striking contrast to "the sternness of the earlier Christian thought which saw Jesus as the repre-sentative of suffering humanity, bearing the punishment for men's sins, and more as the King of Glory paying the ransom to redeem mankind from the devil's power." [10] The origin and the fading of these flashes of the light of Jesus' humanity are difficult to explain. Peculiar social conditions must have provided the opportunity for free-dom of expression. They did not penetrate the formal statements of the doctrine of the church, but these songs and pictures must have formed and colored the unspoken impression that generations of men and women from that time to this have had of Jesus. Songs, stories, and pictures are the most powerful means of arousing interest in someone as a human being. The medieval ones spoke of humanity, love, and joy. The prolific paintings of Jesus in the fifteenth, sixteenth, and seventeenth centuries reinforced on European minds the impression of the human life of Jesus. Their constant choice of two topics—Jesus as an infant with his family and Jesus as a man dying on the cross—have made the birth and death of Jesus the events in his life best known to men.

This interest in the human Jesus, both child and man, which overflowed from the new life of the late Middle Ages into the life of the Reformation and the Counter-Reformation, arose out of the need to find guidance and comfort in the new domestic, economic, and intellectual society that was emerging. It had reactionary tendencies in the desire of some to maintain medieval asceticism, with the crucifix as its symbol, but it also took a new and joyful form in the desire to find Jesus in the demands and comforts of family life. This was expressed in the paintings of the Holy Family and in the devotion that the Counter-Reformation centered on it. In the Reformed Church there was the same interest in the family, probably indeed a stronger interest, but it was expressed more intellectually and therefore more austerely in the reading of the Bible. All through the church the ferment of the time inspired a new desire to know more about Jesus. It was an uncertain picture, but it was powerful just because it was a picture, and it's still the picture that many people have of Jesus.

Through the rebels and the heretics

It was by no means only the devout who showed an interest in Jesus and a desire to know more about him. This interest was perhaps even more noticeable among critics inside and opponents outside the church. Those who were more than dissatisfied with what the church was doing were apt to turn to Jesus for support. Michael Servetus, who was executed at Geneva in 1553 for heresy, claimed that Jesus was gentle and taught the Christian to offer the other cheek and to be merciful and charitable. Sebastian Castellio was so shocked by Servetus' execution that he published a manifesto in favor of toleration. In it these words occur: "O Christ, creator and king of the world, dost thou see? Art thou become quite other than thyself, so cruel, so contrary to thyself? When thou didst live upon earth, none was more gentle, more merciful, more patient of wrong. . . . Men scourged thee, spat upon thee, crowned thee with thorns, crucified thee among thieves and thou didst pray for them who did this wrong. Art thou now so changed? . . . If thou, O Christ, hast commanded these executions and tortures, what hast thou left for the devil to do?" [11] This point of view was to be found also among such groups as the Moravians.

Nor was it only the dissentients inside the church who claimed to know Jesus and to find in their knowledge of him the proper guide to their actions. The same point of view was expressed by some who would have little to do with the church and indeed opposed it. When toleration had been to some extent achieved and men began to organize themselves in their own independent political, economic, and cultural societies, they still claimed to know Jesus. They repudiated the church. They did not repudiate Jesus. Indeed they claimed that he was on their side.

This claim was strongly evident among deists and free-thinkers in the eighteenth century. Thomas Jefferson, third President of the United States, can represent them. He had no love of the church and the church had no love of him. "To the corruptions of Christianity I am, indeed, opposed; but not to the genuine precepts of Jesus. I am a Christian in the only sense in which he wished anyone to be; sincerely attached to his doctrines, in preference to all others ascribing to himself very human excellence; and believing that he never claimed any other." [12] Elsewhere he wrote of the importance of the teachings of Jesus "in inculcating universal philanthropy, not only to kindred and friends, to neighbours and countrymen, but to all mankind, gathering all in one family, under the bonds of love, charity, peace, common wants and common aids." [13] These opinions, which we tend to associate with this century rather than two hundred years ago, had a profound effect on the molding of political and religious thinking in America and elsewhere. They are based on and assume a knowledge about Jesus that could not have been taken for granted much earlier. It is easy to dismiss this picture as inadequate and too simple, but it indicates how some men claimed to know about Jesus and how important they felt this knowledge to be. And it is probable that this picture was more influential than many a good churchman's just because it was expressed in ordinary language, political rather than theological.

In the eighteenth century this political view of Jesus

was expressed articulately by many sophisticated and ed-
ucated people. A hundred years later it was expressed
more vehemently by representatives of the workers of
Great Britain and America. The incipient labor movement in Great Britain, disgusted with the church's lack
of interest in the condition of the working population,
founded what they called "labor churches." These were
vehemently antichurch and antitheology. But they were
not anti-Jesus. One newspaper in 1891 reported that there
"was a loud burst of applause which greeted the name of
Jesus when it was first mentioned in the afternoon service by Mr. Ben Tillett." Three years later another paper
wrote: "It was a sound instinct that made the Socialists
of America at a recent meeting cheer every allusion to
Christ." And "cheers for Jesus were a common thing at
Labour meetings in Britain and elsewhere." [14]

Both Jefferson and the labor movement felt that
Jesus spoke to their condition. It was concern about their
own condition and that of their country that stimulated
their desire to know Jesus and helped them to see him as
a person. It is salutary to remember that men's interest in
Jesus has depended on the political and theological rebels
as much as on the orthodox. We want to know about
someone only if we feel that he can speak to our condition. So it is not surprising that it has often been the
rebels who have kept the knowledge of Jesus alive in the
hearts and minds of men when the church seemed to be
saying very little.

Through the scholars

Today the situation is different: The members of the church and the general population of the West probably know more about Jesus than in any previous age. Our shock at reported ignorance about Jesus among children and young people is an indication of how much we take for granted that a full knowledge about him is available and has been supplied to all. This could not have been taken for granted in any previous century except, perhaps, in the last century in some places.

This has been due to the work of scholars in the second half of the last century and the first half of this. They set out to discover all that could be known about Jesus. It is difficult for us today to realize how new this study is and how refreshing. We forget how little the preaching and teaching of the church has had to do with the life of Jesus and his teaching. It has had to do with doctrine stated in abstract terms. But what inspired this new quest for knowledge about Jesus? Men were being brought into a new, free, democratic way of life. They were facing new national and social problems. Science was questioning the origin of man, and politics was questioning his destiny. This concern about man made men interested in the man Jesus. It was no merely academic study that pushed the scholars on. They wanted to understand Jesus so that they might understand themselves and the life they were being called to live. Scholarly interest in Jesus was part of the new social concern of the church. And, of course, the springs of this interest go farther back and deeper down. They go back at least to the French Revolution and the romantic movement.

The prophetic theological figure is Schleiermacher, the German theologian at the end of the eighteenth and the beginning of the nineteenth centuries. While Europe was reeling under Napoleon, Schleiermacher challenged the hold of traditional dogmatic theology and sent men down new lines of thought and feeling. He had inherited from the Moravians a lively interest in the person of Jesus. In the chaos of the times men wanted to understand their own human experience. It was this that impelled them to try to find out all they could about the Jesus of history.

Men's quest has inevitably led them into all kinds of theories and methods of interpretation. There has been no general agreement but plenty of controversy. Their conclusion seemed to be that we could never hope to get back to indisputable facts. They claimed that a final, definitive life of Jesus could never be written, but this only set off more men on the task of writing his life. More "lives of Jesus" have been written since then than ever before, but this was healthy and to be expected. We owe a tremendous debt of gratitude to the scholars who have cleared away a great deal of theological clutter and let us see Jesus. Perhaps we owe as great a debt to their lack of agreement. The unscholarly man is not put off by being told that the scholars cannot be sure of the facts and do not agree among themselves. In a way this makes Jesus all the more like someone they can know. The people they do know well in their ordinary lives have their mysteries that cannot be explained. They know them without having to verify all the facts. If the scholars cannot agree, then they, as ordinary men, have as good a right to their own opinions. And these are the only grounds on which we can come to know anyone.

The classic book on the subject, *The Quest of the Historical Jesus,* by Albert Schweitzer, ends with a paragraph that was almost too widely quoted fifty years ago but that does sum up the conclusion of many, both scholars and ordinary people, that, if the Jesus of history is elusive, the Jesus of experience is still here for us to know: "He comes to us as One unknown, without a name, as of old, by the lake-side, He came to those men who knew Him not. He speaks to us the same word: 'Follow thou me!' and sets us to the tasks which He has to fulfil for our time. He commands. And to those who obey Him, whether they be wise or simple, He will reveal Himself in the toils, the conflicts, the sufferings which they shall pass through in His fellowship and, as an ineffable mystery, they shall learn in their own experience Who He is." [15]

We know about Jesus through the experience of other men and women—through innumerable other men and women. The Gospels are basic to our knowing about Jesus: what he did and what he said and the impact he made on those who knew him. It is through their experience and only through their experience that we can learn these facts. The experience of those down the centuries who have claimed to know him has also been essential for us. They have come to know about him in the conditions of their own time. Without their experience we would not be in the position of wanting to know or being able to know anything about him. They have passed it on to us. If we have been fortunate, we have known one or two persons for whom knowing about Jesus was the supreme thing in their lives. We may have been infected with their interest or at least aroused to curiosity. But from the general experience of men which has formed that corporate knowledge about Jesus which is part of our social heritage we can isolate the three lines that we have been considering. There are, first, the devout, who include the artists as well as those engaged in worship. Then there are the rebels who are moved by love or hate; and, as Albert Schweitzer pointed out, you need to have either love or hate to break through the shams to historical insight.[16] And, lastly, there are the scholars who, if they are to help us to see, need to have a touch of both the artist and the rebel. Without these three groups we would find it difficult to know about Jesus and even to read the records.

But the acquiring of this knowledge about Jesus is something that we have to do for ourselves. And even when we have attained it, can we claim to know Jesus? Or do we only know about him? Should we ask for more?

"KNOWING"
AND "KNOWING ABOUT"

The difference

The twelve disciples knew Jesus through personal contact. They shared their daily life with him, eating with him, fishing with him, listening to him, talking to him, wondering at his silences, mystified by his way of treating other people. They knew his voice, his touch, his mind. They knew him, as we know our friends, by the intonation of his voice, by the movement of his hands, by his way of walking, by his smile. Such knowledge is not acquired quickly. It cannot be hurried. It cannot be attained vicariously. It depends on the mutual sharing of time and space. No one since then has known this intimate, personal experience of Jesus.

Since then men have known about Jesus. They have known about him because those who knew him in this intimate way felt that they must put on record what they knew of him and what this knowledge had meant to them. As a result, men in all ages have known about Jesus and thought about him. Some have put on record their reactions to him and their relationship to him, and we today know about him mainly because the church has formed a continuous succession of men and women committed to his name and, therefore, has preserved knowledge of him.

The contrast between the twelve disciples and all other Christians is clear. It is the same as that between the disciples of Plato and those who since his time have studied his writings, or between Napoleon's staff and those who study his campaigns now.

The distinction between "knowing" and "knowing about" would seem to be absolute.

Yet, when we inquire a little more deeply, the distinction loses its clear-cut edge. It is difficult to draw the distinction according to the different results of "knowing" and "knowing about." Immediate personal contact may be very superficial. Indirect knowledge, based on dedicated interest and sustained study, may lead to more profound knowledge. We may feel we don't really know someone whom we meet every day. If we have read Sir Walter Scott's *Journal*, we may well feel that we know him as intimately as we know many of our acquaintances. Indeed, Edward Gibbon, author of *The Decline and Fall of the Roman Empire*, claimed that he knew Homer best of all his friends. Yet the difference certainly remains. We might say that it is the difference between knowing firsthand and knowing secondhand, or the difference between knowing people and knowing about facts or things.

The difference: Is it between
knowing people and knowing about facts?

There is an obvious difference between the way in which we look at people and the way in which we look at things. We can deal with things as objects. We can measure them and test them and know all about them, but we can't deal with people in this way. There is something in them—life—that we can never measure or test or know all about. But this is too simple. We have at times to treat people as objects. We have to count them, as inhabitants of a town, the members of an age group or an income group. We cannot plan for social welfare in housing, schools, and hospitals without numbering people. We don't resent it. We know that it is necessary and we do it with ourselves. We assess our own needs and the needs of our families. We can do so only by measuring our needs and gathering facts about ourselves. In other words we treat ourselves as objects. We are aware that there is a danger of going beyond this. We can treat people solely as things, as objects to be used, or as objects to be eliminated when we drop bombs on them or starve them.

But this does not take us very far in drawing a line of distinction between "knowing" and "knowing about." For one thing, as soon as we know something about the people we are bombing or starving, we can no longer go on treating them heedlessly as things. By knowing something about them we have awakened to the fact that they are people whom we could know. We generally need to know something about people in order to get to know them. On the other hand, our way of regarding things is neither uniform nor unchanging, nor is it even always impersonal. We know what a tree is. We may know a lot about trees, but we may look at a particular tree in a quite different way from the way in which we look at other trees. We may have planted it. We may have seen it grow year by year. We may have seen how it reacts to storm or drought. We may know a lot about it and may even claim to know it in a personal way. When we come to think of a painting or a statue or a piece of music or a poem, our attitude is again quite different. It is not enough to see it as canvas or bronze or paper, for this is not what it is. It may appear to be only this until we realize that it expresses the thought and imagination of some person, set in material form so that others may derive some pleasure or meaning from it. We do not need to know the person who made it. We do not need to know anything about him. It may come to mean so much to us that we may claim to "know" the painting or the statue, the music or the poem, in much the same way as we know a friend, but we can do this only insofar as we bring to our seeing some touch of knowing that is akin to the way in which we know people. It may well be that this personal commitment is necessary for knowing anything, person or thing, for knowing is a personal activity. It is something I do.

So it is difficult to make the dividing line between "knowing" and "knowing about" lie in the distinction between persons and things, people and facts.

Or is it between
firsthand and secondhand knowledge?

We may feel that the distinction is between firsthand and secondhand. We "know" someone through face-to-face encounter, firsthand. We "know about" someone through hearing others speak of him or through reading about him, secondhand. But is not this too clear-cut? Do we know anything absolutely firsthand? Can we know any person or any thing without the meditation of another person or without the help of things that we see or hear or touch? We might say that a baby's knowledge of his mother is basic, firsthand knowledge, but it is based on touch. The infant has to find out something "about" his mother. He has to learn that she is near and warm and gives him food before he can begin the process of knowing her. Indeed, his basic knowledge is this physical contact. We cannot know anyone unless we are somehow brought into contact with him. It may be through the simplest of sensory contacts or through the formal introduction of a friend. We see him and are interested in him, or we hear someone talk about him, or we find, to our surprise, that he is interested in us. There needs to be some kind of contact of sight or sound or mind before we can take a step toward knowing him.

It seems almost impossible to disentangle "knowing" from "knowing about." We cannot know someone without knowing something about him. We cannot know about him without being on the way to knowing him. "Knowing" is primary in importance but not in time. As David Cairns wisely writes: "This first kind of knowledge,

'knowledge of,' is prior to the second, 'knowledge about.' Not always necessarily prior in time, for I can know a lot about a man before I meet him. But prior in many senses, one of the chief of which is that the great proportion of our knowledge about persons is ultimately derived from our own or other people's knowledge 'of' these persons. 'Knowledge of' cannot occur without an increase of 'knowledge about,' and these two kinds of knowledge are extremely interwoven in our experience." [17]

This means that a clear distinction between firsthand and secondhand knowledge is not easy to maintain. We quite inevitably think that what we see with our own eyes has far more authority than what other people tell us they see. It is not just the vain feeling that we are much less likely to have made a mistake. It is much more the feeling that what we know directly has a pristine freshness that is denied to what we learn secondhand. It is a useful prejudice if it makes us careful to look at things for ourselves, but it must not disguise from us the fact that practically all our knowledge comes to us secondhand. For it we depend on other people. As Michael Polanyi says: "The overwhelming part of our factual beliefs are held at secondhand through trusting others; and in the great majority of cases our trust is placed in the authority of certain persons, either by virtue of their public office or as our chosen intellectual leaders." [18] Most of the assumptions on which we base the living of our lives are taken on trust. The modern technological pattern of our lives depends on our trust in scientific knowledge far beyond our comprehension. Without this trust we would be lost. No one, not even the most learned scientist, knows everything. The whole structure of scientific knowledge rests on the mutual acceptance of the knowledge of innumerable other people—on their acceptance and on their continued questioning. This is true of every part of our lives. We may feel that there is a portion of our lives, and the most important portion, in which we see for ourselves and act on our own judgment, but even here we depend for the basis of our judgment on what we have learned from others. Our experience cannot be separated from the experience of other people. For most of us and in most matters our knowledge is not even secondhand. It goes back much farther.

If this applies, as it certainly does, to our understanding of the world in which we live, it applies even more unquestionably to our knowledge of the past. Our knowledge of the past can be mediated to us only through the experience of men and women of innumerable generations. If we are not particularly interested in the past and would gladly be rid of it, we can do so only as we realize that our opinions and our attitudes, our patterns of living, and even our wish to rebel are inherited and are formed by the experience of those who lived in the past. We can say that the past is dead, but even if we wish to repudiate it, we can't escape from it. Even if rebellion is the only thing that has meaning for us, the things against which we rebel are inherited from the past. The past determines the object and the nature of our rebellion. We can never dismiss anything as of secondary value because it comes to us secondhand. We never dare claim that anything we do is our own unaided work.

It thus seems impossible to draw a clear line of distinction between "knowing" and "knowing about." The difference between people and things doesn't help much. The distinction between first- and secondhand doesn't get us very far, yet we would all recognize that there is a clear difference between the flash of understanding that convinces me that I know someone and the slow accumulation of information that enables me in the end to claim that I know something about him. Despite our difficulty in defining it, there remains this intrinsic difference.

Or is the difference between looking to the past and looking to the future?

One possible distinction remains: the distinction between the past and the future. All our knowledge "about" persons and things comes from the past. Our experience is what we have learned in the past. A great deal of our experience is based on corporate knowledge that goes far back into the remote past—all the things that we take for granted—the certainty that night follows day and winter summer, all our fears, our joys, our hopes. Our own personal experience, however direct and illuminating it may be, once we have known it, belongs to the past—to an immediately recent past but still the past. The word I have just typed, the bird I have just seen flying past the window, the thought that has just occurred to me—these have now all slipped into the past. Most are beyond the recall of conscious memory, but, even though forgotten, they are part of my experience. Any knowledge that I have of life and of the world, of other people and of myself, any wisdom and any ability to live—all these depend on past experience, immediate or remote, remembered or forgotten.

We know about the past. On our knowledge of it we form our judgments and base our actions. We do not know about the future. We, indeed, act on the assumption that the future will continue the line of the past, but we know that this is by no means certain. We know that anything may happen to us, to other people, to the world. The future is unpredictable. We can never be sure of it. To meet it we have to make choices, take decisions, and run risks.

I am confronting the future all the time. But in a quite definite way I confront the future whenever I meet someone. Whenever I come to know someone, I enter an unpredictable world. I do not know how he will affect me or I him. This is the intrinsic difference between "knowing" a person and "knowing about" him. Knowledge about a person is knowledge of facts. It is knowledge about the past, and without some such knowledge I cannot attain to the stage of knowing him. But this knowing him is something intrinsically different. It is not inevitable. I can avoid it. It cannot be measured. It cannot be tested. It cannot be explained. It belongs to the future.

This kind of knowing, which is the acceptance of the uncertainty of the future, is not seen only in the way we know other people. We see it also in the artist's creative response to a new vision and in the scientist's leap into a new discovery. If we are ruled by the past, we can do nothing. To encounter the future is to be in some way creative. The business of knowing a person is a matter of creativity because it is a step into the future, but it is not inevitably the result of face-to-face encounter.

This difference between looking to the past and looking to the future marks the distinction between "knowing about" and "knowing," but even here we must not make the distinction too rigid. In all knowing, whether it be knowing of or knowing about, there is an element of looking to the future. Knowing is one activity, not two. In any kind of knowing there must be an element of interest or curiosity or fear, and each is based on the uncertainty of the future. Curiosity or anxiety or interest or a sense of need has to be aroused if we are to know about anything. Our ability to know depends on our being persons standing on the razor-edge between the past and the future, learning from past experience what to expect but aware all the time that what we expect is never certain to happen, that life means change.

"Knowing" and "knowing about": contrasts and comparisons

Any kind of knowing is a personal activity. It is something I do. I have to choose to know someone or to know about some person or some thing. And I have to decide to do something to make my choice actual.

Life, indeed, is a business of making choices and taking decisions. Our daily choices and decisions may have become so habitual that we forget we have ever made them. So we are apt to feel that everything is determined for us. It is true that we had no choice of the family into which we were born, and for the majority of the world's inhabitants there is no choice as to where they live and what they do each day. What distinguishes life in our Western developed society is the extent to which choice is open to us. But, indeed, even for those who live in the most limited of societies there is choice: the choice of how to live and with whom. As Sidney Jourard writes: "Every man chooses his way of being in the world. But I would go further and assert that people choose their way of being *for somebody.*" [19] In other words, everyone makes some choice, conscious or unconscious, effective or otherwise, as to how he is going to live his daily life, and this choice depends to a great extent on the person—parent, wife, husband, child, friend—whom he knows in a close personal relationship. Whom we know and how we know them are choices that are always up to us. It may be that we make no choices. But this is our choice.

In getting to know someone I commit myself. In the case of face-to-face meeting, commitment is obvious. It is confirmed by the response of him whom I have met. Getting to know someone is a mutual business. I cannot know him unless he knows me, and once I know him I can never free myself. I can, of course, quarrel with him. I may refuse to see him. If I am married to him, I can get a divorce. Mutual circumstances may mean that we never have a chance of meeting. But whatever happens, I can never cut my knowledge of him out of my life, and, fortunately, I don't generally want to. My knowledge of him remains always an enriching factor in my life.

To get to know someone in the past is a different business. There can be commitment. There cannot be response. There has, indeed, to be the commitment of desire, intention, and application if I am to get to know someone in the past. It will all depend on my work. He makes no response. He cannot help me. But neither can I offend him. I can leave him quite alone for any length of time. I can then resume the acquaintance whenever I want without any excuse or estrangement.

In both cases there is risk. You cannot know beforehand where friendship will lead you. You cannot control the outcome of knowing someone. Your knowledge of him may shed a new light on life and the way to live it. It may awaken you to new desires and new ambitions. Your life may take a new direction. This is indubitable in the case of flesh and blood friends, but it also can happen through our interest in someone in the past. As we saw, interest in Tolstoi led Howells into socialism, and many a man has been inspired to choose a career or a way of life through admiration of someone whom he has read about and come to know intimately.

"All knowledge of persons is by revelation." [20] This marks the difference between knowing people and knowing things. In getting to know someone I am not just gathering information about him. I don't just find what I am looking for, because I don't know what I'm looking for. The joy of getting to know someone is that we find something unexpected, something surprising, certainly something that does not owe anything to our seeking. It is something that comes to me out of the very being of my friend. He discloses himself to me without knowing that he does so, as I presumably disclose myself to him. Without intention "I disclose myself in many ways—in words, by my actions, gestures, and facial expressions, by my omissions—all these acts reveal my aims, my feelings and attitudes, my beliefs, my memories of the past." [21] This disclosing of a person can be neither contrived nor explained. It can only be called revelation. Our response is akin to our appreciation of a painting or a bit of music or our sense of beauty in a landscape or the flash of understanding of some truth. We know that it is there, that it is true, that we have had nothing to do with it, that it speaks directly to us, and that reason has nothing to do with it.

Most of us have known this sense of revelation in meeting a person for the first time or in slowly getting to know him. Without it life would be bleak. There is no doubt that this awareness of something revealed can come to us also from learning about someone in the past. Through our study of him and through our identifying ourselves with him, he is revealed to us in a way that sets some truth alight and brings new meaning and hope into life. We cannot understand the age-long influence and attraction of men like Socrates or Luther without realizing that they have the power still to reveal something of themselves to men today.

In the case of both those whom we know intimately and those of the past whom we choose and contrive to know, we are led by our knowledge of them into a new freedom. It is the freedom of a wider world of other people. Most of us know something of this freedom which comes to us from knowing a particular person—

wife or husband, child or friend. It has led us into a more confident attitude toward life, to a greater understanding of other people, to a less fearful view of ourselves, to a strange new sense of unity with other men. Many of us would claim that the excitement of getting to know someone from the past has the same effect though in a more intellectual form. Despite the fact that it is a one-way relationship, I find myself responding to him in unexpected ways. My life is never quite the same again. He has set me on a new line of thought and action. He has confronted me with my own future and the future of the world through the revelation of how he confronted his future and the future of his world. The result of knowing him has not been so very different from the effect of knowing my flesh-and-blood friend. It may even be more difficult for me to resist my response to him, just because I have had to work for it myself.

The similarity lies in the effect that "knowing" and "knowing about" have on myself. In both cases I am involved in decision, choice, response to revelation, action, and unity. I have been brought into the world of other people or, at least, of one other person. I realize that I live in the present where past and future meet. Abraham Maslow, the American humanist philosopher, speaks in one of his books of his sense of identification with the long procession of teachers leading up to himself. He then adds: "This kind of transcendence of time is also true in another sense, namely, that I can feel friendly, in a very personal and affectionate way, with Spinoza, Abraham Lincoln, Jefferson, William James, Whitehead, etc., as if they still lived. Which is to say that in specific ways they *do* still live." [22] They live still for him. And this is what matters for him. For him, through affection and work, "knowing about" and "knowing" have become one.

"Knowing about" Jesus and "knowing" Jesus

We know about Jesus in the same way that we know about anyone else in the past. We know about him from the records that his contemporaries kept. We know about him from what men and women down the centuries and in varying circumstances have said about him and thought about him, have sung about him, and from the ways in which they have painted him. We have known about him because we are worried about the life we live and find that he comes into our life with question, rebuke, and command. The difference between our knowledge of him and our knowledge of anyone else from the past is that there is so much more to know about him and that it touches our life at so many points. There is no doubt that at different times and in divergent situations men and women have found him to have something to say to their condition. Through knowing about him they have seen themselves, other men, and the world in a new light. They have found liberty, joy, and a new direction to their lives. Many would claim that in knowing about him they have come to know him as they know their other friends. Many would say more than this. They would say that because they know him, they know that he is as much alive now as when he walked on earth.

When they say this, do they mean more than what Maslow meant when he wrote that his favorite philosophers "*do* still live" for him? Most would say that they mean more than this. But if we mean more, we must at least mean this. Any further claim on our part means nothing at all unless we mean at least, and as passionately, what Maslow meant. There is no point in our saying that Jesus still lives unless we know that in our own lives we have made him live for us. And we cannot say this unless we on our part fulfill Maslow's two conditions. We must regard Jesus with personal affection, and we must be trying to live his life, just as Maslow was following the profession of his predecessors. In the end, is not this the only way we get to know someone—by liking him and working with him?

There are those who would say that this is their position. This is as far as they can honestly go. They know Jesus and seek to know him better. They see him as giving meaning and hope to their lives and to the lives of other men. This is an honest position. Those who hold it have every right to claim that they know Jesus and not just know about him.

But many would go farther than this. Their reason for doing so is not just that they are suspicious of so subjective a line. Perhaps they would welcome some objective, extraneous proof. In the end, however, their objection arises out of their own experience, which is as well, for we are in a realm where there can be no objective, extraneous proof.

Some in all ages would claim that they know Jesus because of some experience that goes beyond reading and hearing and thinking. In some way that they would not attempt to explain they believe that Jesus has appeared to them or spoken to them personally. Paul's conversion on the road to Damascus is the classic case. No one has the facts or can have the facts to make an objective study of it. We have only Paul's repeated description of it. We have no reason to doubt his experience, but we have only his subjective description. What we can say with some definiteness is that if Paul had not known about Jesus, if he had not been hysterically intent on silencing his opponents, if—as is possible—he could not get rid of the memory of having seen Jesus, perhaps on the cross, he could not have received a vision of him. The business of knowing a person affects the whole of a man's life. It obliterates any clear division between subjective and objective.

Behind any claim to have a mystical experience of Jesus must lie this primary, rudimentary knowledge of Jesus. But there must be more. A man must be so convinced of him, either in agreement or in opposition, that he is prepared, and even expects, to hear him speak through the events of his own life and the lives of other people. He must believe that he holds a key place in the destiny of men. There can be no overwhelming experience without this prior knowledge.

For the first disciples, and for many since, the resurrection has been the undeniable proof that they can know Jesus now. This is not the place to discuss the nature of the resurrection appearances of Jesus. It is possible to get so involved in the interpretation of Bible passages and so committed to pseudoscientific explanations that we wander far from the facing of the fundamental question of how we know Jesus in the world today. But there are some things we should remember.

First, it is well to remember the concluding words of Jesus' parable of Dives and Lazarus: "If they hear not Moses and the prophets, neither will they be persuaded, though one rose from the dead" (Luke 16:31). Jesus seems to be implying that any kind of belief founded on a miracle, even such an incredible miracle as a man's rising from the dead, was not the kind of belief that mattered. It had to be learned in the hard business of living.

Secondly, the condition for knowing that he had overcome death and was alive forever was quite different. In the records there is no case of anyone having this experience who did not already know him and was forever committed to him in affection. Only those who loved Jesus knew that he was risen. This is not to doubt the essential truth of their experience. It may seem to be getting back into a subjective world, where men see what they want to see. It is, rather, that we are pulled back all the time to the basic question of what we mean by "knowing." What do we mean by knowing anyone? What do we mean by knowing Jesus? What do we mean by knowing God? This is the basic question because belief of any kind and the living of any kind of human life depends on our ability to know. It is a personal activity. It is something that we do for ourselves, that no one else can do for us, however much our knowledge depends on their knowledge. Even when we learn from things that happen to us from the outside, we still have to take them in and interpret them for ourselves. We cannot get away from this subjective element in knowledge. Without it we can never talk about knowing Jesus.

The uniqueness of the claim that men make for Jesus is that they can know him now. Knowing about Jesus and knowing Jesus can become one. They become one, not in the acceptance of a doctrine or even in the acceptance of a fact, but in our experience of a life and our confidence that in that life is the only meaning of life and the only hope of the world. We do not know the destiny of the world. We have no explanation of life. But we do know him now.

In the fellowship of the Spirit

In the New Testament it is never suggested that only those who have had a personal experience of the resurrection could properly be called Christians. Indeed, it was regarded as so exceptional an experience that Paul could count up the number of cases and assume that his own, which others questioned, was the last. The essential condition for being a Christian was put quite differently. It was in knowing Jesus. Put more particularly, it was in knowing Jesus as Lord, and such knowledge was by the Spirit.

To know someone is an activity of the human spirit. It depends on mutual sympathy and understanding, on the sense of being made of the same stuff and yet each being unique. In the simplest friendship between two persons these two factors must be present, but they point far beyond the simple fact of a casual friendship. They illustrate basic attitudes to life and the world. In trusting myself to sympathy with another person, I am expressing my belief in life. We trust the world because we trust another person and in our expectation that he will do something unexpected, we are expressing our belief that there is a purpose and a meaning in life. To know someone is to commit oneself to the future.

But there is only one Spirit, as Paul wrote. The human spirit by which we know one another and can communicate is the same as the creative Spirit of all life. It is manifestly the same Spirit by which we know Jesus. When the first Christians asserted that their faith was that Jesus is Lord and that they could say this only through the Spirit, they were asserting these two things. They were not saying that they would give Jesus a title or even that he was their leader. They were asserting that in him they knew the meaning of all things, that in him the purpose of the world and the meaning of human life were to be found. They were also asserting that it was only through faith in the unity of the Spirit that they could believe and hold onto this.

In saying that Jesus is Lord they were making the stupendous assertion that Jesus holds the key to physical existence. They were stating emphatically what we hint at tentatively when we say that we know someone as a friend. They were committing themselves to life and to the future. In saying that it was only by the Spirit that men could know Jesus, Paul was saying that they shared a common spirit with Jesus and with all other men. The spirit that was manifest in him and that they now recognized in themselves was the creative Spirit at work in the world. It was by this one Spirit that they had learned to know about Jesus. It was the same Spirit that would lead them into fuller truth. The Spirit was one. It was the source of unity and the bond of fellowship. It was the spirit of Jesus. In the church it was known to them in its fruits and in their obedience, but it was the creative Spirit of all things. By it all men lived, even though they did not recognize it. We would get much closer to what the New Testament means by the Spirit if we called it the common spirit rather than the Holy Spirit. For the word "holy" has come to mean for us almost everything that the Spirit was not: separate, detached, peculiar, remote. The original meaning of the word "holy" had to do with wholeness and health, with what was undivided, perfect, common. The Spirit cannot divide men. It can only unite. It is indeed the means of all unity among men.

We cannot discuss knowing Jesus without talking about the Spirit. We cannot make some vision or mystical experience the condition for knowing Jesus, though this is not to deny such experiences. We cannot regard willingness to accept some physical or metaphysical explanation of the resurrection experiences of the first disciples as a means of knowing Jesus. We can never escape from the discussion of them. And such discussion can help us to know more about the first disciples and so know something more about Jesus.

There is only one condition to our knowing Jesus: that we recognize the one common spirit linking him and us and all men. This is why in the early church those who had come to know Jesus spoke so confidently about the Spirit. This was also the reason why they were so sure that all men everywhere would be brought into his purpose, God's purpose for the world. This in the end was why they could speak with utter confidence about the future. Without the Spirit we cannot talk about purpose and destiny, about glory and truth, about the mystery of love and suffering.

It is because of the Spirit that we can dare to talk about knowing Jesus now and not just about knowing about him. But, of course, we have first to know about him, just as we have to get to know something about our contemporary friends before we begin to know them personally. This business of knowing about Jesus demands intention and application. This is all the more necessary because we in the West cannot avoid participating in a vague, dispersed knowledge about Jesus that often gives him the distortion of a caricature. We begin to acquire a personal knowledge of him when we bring concern about our own situation in the world into our attempt to know him. Our knowledge of him becomes truly personal when we accept that the Spirit calls us to take risks for the sake of an unknown future. If we fail in this, our knowledge of Jesus becomes academic and static. This can happen in our relationships with our other friends. We can become possessive of them and afraid of anything that threatens change in our relations with them. We become afraid of anything that might separate us or that threatens the exclusiveness of our relationship. We become afraid of absence and terrified of death. We stop living. We stop learning to know our friend and ourself and life. We deny the Spirit. And the same is true of our knowledge of Jesus.

Even when we are sure that we can know him now in

our present life, we are only at the beginning of the business of knowing him. The process of knowing him never ends. It takes the whole of life, and there are two steps that are necessary: we have to learn to know him in action, and we have to learn to know him with and through other people.

CHAPTER

4

IN ACTION

We get to know people through doing things

In youth we are wide-ranging in the choice of our friends. Curiosity, the desire to make contacts outside our family, and the exhilarating joy of making new friends make us adventurous.

Later, when we are tied to the responsibilities of a job and a home of our own, we are content with a more restricted range. The friends we make then are not of our choosing but sometimes our knowledge of them goes much deeper. We make our friends then from among those with whom we work. Common work, not curiosity, is what leads us to know them. In working on a job that we cannot escape, with others whom we cannot avoid, we often come to know them and to be known by them in a more fundamental way than in our leisure or cultural life. In our self-chosen activities we can play a role and assume a part and hide ourselves. We cannot do this so easily in the daily sharing of a common job. It is this sharing together in work that cements a marriage. This inescapable, mutual knowledge is peculiarly obvious where there is great difficulty or danger or where success or survival depends on mutual responsibility. This is evident in mountaineering, space exploration, or war.

"Comrade" and "companion," the old words for those whom a man knew well, expressed this bond of common and hard work. "Comrade" originally meant the sharer of a room or a tent or a bed. "Companion" originally meant the sharer of bread. A comrade or a companion is one who shares bed or board, tent or bread, because he shares a hard job in life. And your comrade or companion is the one you really know. You realize the demands you can make on him and he can make on you. These are the circumstances in which we really get to know another person. We are not trying to get to know him. We are tied together in the doing of a common job. We are not primarily interested in each other. We are more likely to be concerned to see that we can succeed in doing what we've got to do. In action we get to know each other.

This was the way in which the twelve disciples came to know Jesus. To share bed and board was the first demand he made of them. This was what marked them off from others who made glad but casual contact with him. The disciples had to share the hardness of his life, in which they had nowhere to lay their heads and never knew where their next meal was coming from. They found the going pretty hard. They probably did not at first feel that they were getting to know him any better through this kind of life. They seem to have felt that he had become more difficult to understand. Before they left all to follow him, they had shared with the others a simple, clear picture of what he was like and of what they hoped he would do. This picture became blurred for them by the strange things he did and by the questions raised in their minds, yet they were certainly getting to know him by sharing his daily life, by seeing how he treated other people, by observing how he looked at simple things like flowers and birds, by his silences when they expected him to speak, and by the strange things he said when he did speak. They were learning that to know someone does not always mean to understand him.

He also gave them things to do on their own, without him. He sent them to feed the five thousand. He sent them out two by two to meet people without allowing them to make any preparations for their journey. He sent two to take possession of someone's donkey. No action that he demanded of them was easy. Each action raised questions in their minds. And, in the end, their actions looked like involving them in acute personal danger that they could not face. The business of knowing him committed them to doing things that were uncomfortable, never quite intelligible, and rarely exactly welcome. They must often have felt that they would prefer to be left to watch him doing things, to admire, to ask questions, and to criticize. Perhaps they would have liked to claim more time to get to know him before they committed themselves to action. But would they have got to know him?

Is not this an indication of the way by which we get to know our friends? We would often find it hard to say how we first got in touch with them or how our friendship really began. Most of us have had the happy experience of meeting someone and finding, perhaps immediately that life had taken on a new meaning and a richness unknown before. Usually this revelation came when we did something with him or her and talk gave place to action. In doing something together life seemed to blossom and bring strange new but welcome demands, new relationships with other people, and a new light on the future. This experience probably happens once or twice to most people and is one of the greatest joys that life brings. Certainly to most of the twelve disciples, if not to all, this was what meeting Jesus must have meant.

We get to know people even through opposition

But it is not always like this. There are other friends whom we make and with whom our experiences may be different. In the end we may reap as rich a reward, but the beginning may be hard and going rough. When first we become involved in some activity with someone, we may feel resentment and even fear and be unfriendly and uncooperative. We don't want to get too involved. We are suspicious of him. We are aware that he has other interests, other activities in which he is engaged, other people to whom he is committed, a purpose of his own in life. We are afraid that if we really get to know him, we may find that we become involved in his affairs and that he may make unforeseen demands on us. There are dangers in getting to know anyone. When talk gives place to action, life loses its safe certainty.

Caution may well advise us to draw back. We may feel we must resist. A few, at least, of the disciples felt this at times, and Judas definitely did at the end.

Friendship can even begin in real opposition. We may feel that the last thing we want to do is to become involved with this person who yet fascinates us. Paul is the conspicuous example. He so feared what Jesus had been teaching and what his disciples were still doing in his name that he persecuted them with all the means at his disposal. But persecution can be seen as a perverse form of participation in the actions of another. It implies that you know the other well enough to regard him as a serious danger. You take his activities so seriously that you counter them not just by word but by action. This was clearly the way in which Paul came to know Jesus. In it he was confessing that he did know him, that he had to participate in his actions either by opposing him violently or by giving in. It is difficult for us now to see how otherwise Paul could have come to know Jesus. Certainly Paul regarded it as the only way for him. The other apostles learned to know Jesus through a gradually deepening sharing of his life. This way was closed to Paul, but perhaps this perverse way of getting involved led Paul to know Jesus as fully as any other man has ever done. It was action that brought both the first disciples and then Paul to their full knowledge of Jesus, though the actions were very different.

We today cannot come to know Jesus as his first disciples did through the slow and sometimes bewildering business of sharing daily life with him. It may well be that some of us began with a timid reflection of Paul's violent opposition. Many of us began by being put off Jesus by the way that we in childhood heard people speak of him and by the stories we were told and by the pictures of him that we were supposed to look at. Perhaps children today are in a happier position in that they are aware that there are people who do not want them to know Jesus. We cannot meet Jesus in the flesh. We have first to hear about him from others. Opposition is as likely to awaken our curiosity as blatant propaganda. Our interest has to be aroused, but we begin to know him only when we ourselves begin to do things.

Getting to know Jesus

Through action

What we are discussing is how we learn to know Jesus by the things we do. We are not discussing what we believe about Jesus. We are not discussing what we ought to believe about Jesus or what terms we should use in talking about him. We are not discussing what we should be doing as his disciples in the world today, what kinds of actions are demanded of us. These are important questions and the last one very urgent. But these are not our questions here. We are discussing how we know Jesus and specifically how we get to know him through the things we do. This is the primary question both in time and in importance. Before we can formulate any belief about Jesus we have to know him. Before we can decide what faith in him means for us or what obedience demands of us in action, we have to know him. We have to know whom we are talking about. Otherwise we may well be making his name a pretext for our own opinions. We may be claiming his authority for saying the things we want to say and for doing the things we want to do.

We learn through doing things. Action, if it is our own action and not done in obedience to or in imitation of someone else, demands decision and choice. Of course, obedience and imitation involve decision and choice but not in the nature of the action to be taken. Putting on a tie in the morning demands decision and choice: whether to wear a tie, and, if so, which tie to wear. And decision and choice are often hard. To decide to do one thing means that you decide not to do something else. But life is a matter of choices and decisions. We avoid the daily weight of them through custom and habit. We let others decide for us by falling in with the conventions of our neighbors. We often do all we can to avoid making a choice or coming to a decision, even when we know we ought to. This is probably because when we are young a great deal of pressure is put upon us by home, school, church, and society to submit to their choices and decisions. This pressure is so strong that we have come to make a virtue of indecision and call it "keeping an open mind."

Now learning to live is learning to make our own choices and come to our own decisions. Living creatively means adopting a wider area of choice and a greater depth of decision. "If there were a devil, it would not be one who decided against God, but one who, in eternity, came to no decision." [23] Action is decisive in getting to know someone because it carries the initial choice and decision of wishing to know him into creative response.

When we think of the choices and decisions that confront us whenever we try to decide what we ought to do, we are all too apt to think of the great choices that face us today and the important decisions that we have to make if we are to survive on earth, such as feeding the hungry, reconciling the races, controlling pollution and population. We are uncomfortably aware that these problems are so vast and intractable that individual decision matters nothing at all. We also realize that to get united action throughout the world is beyond any hope based on past experience. There certainly are some final decisions that confront men, but they will be solved only when we and other men have first learned to make decisions on smaller matters. Learning is never a matter of the end but always of the beginning. We learn to make choices in the little first things, not in the final great events. We'll learn to take decisions regarding these only if we have trained ourselves to take decisions first in the lesser choices of daily life.

It is the same in our getting to know a person. We may admire his opinions and the loftiness of his aims and the greatness of his achievements, but it is through his apparently trivial actions that we begin to know him. His ways of doing ordinary things, of looking at people and dealing with them, reveal the particular and unique person he is. We get to know him when our ways of doing things and looking at people change and we are helped to see both him and ourselves better.

This is particularly true in our getting to know Jesus. But there is one great difference between getting to know Jesus and getting to know a contemporary. With someone we can see, it is his actions that are important. With someone whom we cannot see, it is ours that are all-important; so it is by the things we do that we get to know him, not by the things that he does.

Inevitably we begin with trivialities. When we discuss how in our actions we come to know Jesus, we do not begin with the great world-affecting actions to which we think he calls us and in which we feel all Christians should be engaged but are not. Instead, we are thinking of the particular actions of particular people: the things that they do which reflect some kind of decision and choice about Jesus, and we are thinking of the things that we do, not about the things we ought to do.

Through play

We begin with the most elementary—play. Some may think play a too superficial activity to be associated with knowing Jesus, but play is too universal to be dismissed lightly. It is the first activity in which we begin our conscious learning. It is an essential part of our education not only when we are young but all through our life.

Play involves acting a part, pretending we are someone else, doing something that helps us to think ourselves into someone else's life. When a child does it, we call it pretending, but it is a necessary stage of learning for all of us, at all ages. A child learns by imitating an adult. When a father sees his son in play in earnest doing exactly what he does, he learns not only something about his son but something about himself. The son in imitating his father is studying his father and the father in watching his son is studying himself, perhaps for the first time. In the same way when we are much older, we find ourselves doing the things our father did or speaking as he spoke or saying the things he used to say. And we feel that we now know him better than when he was with us. We understand ourselves better because we are unconsciously imitating him. It's an adult extension of a child's play. It should teach us how serious a child's play is.

So in adolescence and later when we have decided that we want to know Jesus, we want to use signs and symbols and gestures to recall us to our intention. To others they may seem a bit of playacting. We wear a badge or a cross. We grow a beard and wear foppish clothes. We may adopt the dress of a medieval monk. Some of us even wear a clerical collar. This may seem very trivial and it has its dangers, especially if it implies a judgment on others, as marking us off as different from them. But in many cases it is a gesture of identification, a pledge to try to know Jesus in ordinary life.

It is, indeed, a simple and almost childish expression of what in more acceptable and sophisticated forms we express in ritual and worship. Christian worship is basically the expression in symbolic action of our participation in the life of Jesus. In the Sacraments we do what he did and what he tells us to do, and we do it in his name. In the profoundest sense we are in worship acting a part in the hope that we may act a better part in ordinary life.

It is the same when we try deliberately to follow the

example and the teaching of Jesus. We do what we think we ought to do in his name: in our care of others, in denial of ourselves, in acceptance of some cause. We want to act the part of his disciples. We do not claim that what we are doing is what we want to do or even what we ourselves would have chosen to do. We want to do what he would do or what he would have us do. In the very best sense of the word we are acting a part, playing as a child plays at being an adult. And we are certainly learning to know Jesus.

It may seem frivolous to call this playacting or to call worship play. But play is the basic means of education, and this is what we are discussing. It is the attempt by imitative action or symbolic gesture to enter into the life of someone else. It is certainly the most common and most elementary way by which in our actions we begin to know someone else. It is an essential first step in our getting to know Jesus.

Through art

The second stage at which we learn to know Jesus through action may seem very different from play—and even more strange. It is not acting, but art. A painter paints a picture of Jesus, for example, Graham Sutherland's painting of the figure of Jesus for the huge tapestry in Coventry Cathedral. A sculptor makes a statue of Jesus as Epstein did for Llandaff Cathedral in Wales. A poet writes a poem about Jesus as Edwin Muir did in "The Transfiguration." What were they doing? Presumably they were trying to translate their seeing of Jesus into line and color, shape and word. Except for the poet, the artist tends not to say much in explanation of what he has created. What he has made is sufficient comment and explanation. Edwin Muir tells in *An Autobiography:* "I had a vague sense during these days that Christ was the turning point of time and the meaning of life to everyone, no matter what his conscious beliefs; to my agnostic friends as well as Christians." [24] The poet is, of course, used to words. He also chooses what he will write a poem about, whereas the painter and the sculptor may be fulfilling commissions. But whatever they are doing and however inarticulate they may be, it is their own creation. They are working out their knowledge of Jesus, interpreting him, expressing their knowledge of him in a way personal to themselves, and in so doing they are coming to be more definite in their knowledge of him. Otherwise their work would have no form. What they do is very different from the work of the scholar. The scholar collects and studies all the available facts and is prepared to give conflicting interpretations of some of them and to state why he prefers one. The artist works quite differently. He has to discard and select until he is left with what appears to him as the essential outline. He cannot give alternate lines or a choice of colors. He must make his choice and stick to it.

This is a process with which most of us have little experience. Few of us have any training as artists, but, more than we realize, we are all untrained artists. We exercise our unskilled craft more than we think. Each one of us has to be a bit of an artist in getting to know our friends. We are always wanting to get a clearer, more living picture of them. We want to see them in clear outline. This is an activity quite different from gathering information about them. Naturally we are interested to know about their past. We want to know what they have done, what have been the determining influences in their lives, what they think now. We want to know all the things we would need to know if we were writing a biography of them. But what we are doing is different. We are drawing a picture of them as we see them really to be. Most of us are very bad at this. We could do it much better if we used our sympathy and imagination more. As Sidney Jourard says: "Artists in society embody and disclose possibilities of experiencing that are available to everyone, but are generally stifled." [25] The material with which we, as artists in ordinary life, have to deal is made up of people. Our ability to know them depends on our seeing them in themselves for ourselves. This business of entering into understanding of other people is one in which we use our minds, our imagination, and our creativity. And because it is a personal activity, it helps me to understand myself better, for I am myself the most difficult person that I have to understand. By discovering another person I discover myself.

This artistic activity is a necessary stage in our coming to know Jesus. Just as we have to draw a mental picture of our friends if we are really to know them, so we have to create our own picture of Jesus if we are to have personal knowledge of him. And our picture will be different from everyone else's. No two painters would paint the same picture of Jesus. No two sculptors would make the same statue. No two poets would write the same poem. They create. They do not imitate. It is the same with the picture we make of Jesus, or of any of our friends. No two people can ever have the same picture of him. We are tempted to think—indeed we are trained to think—that all we need is to have a universal copy—indeed one guaranteed to be accurate—of Jesus for us to recognize and know him. However, that is not how we know anybody. Equally fortunately we can never get it. The four Gospels differ in the pictures they draw of Jesus. No definitive life of Jesus can ever be written. It is up to each one of us to draw his own picture of Jesus, as we do of any of our friends. Most of us will never try to do it on paper. We have to do it in our minds, with our imaginations, if we are ever to know him at all.

Each one of us already has his own picture—vague, childish, sentimental, vivid, or grotesque. If it is to be a living picture, we have to work on it. It is something we do. Dr. Albert Schweitzer probably studied the life of Jesus more fully than anyone else has ever done. The picture he himself drew would now appeal to very few people, but he said two very significant things. The first was that "there is no historical task which so reveals a man's true self as the writing of a Life of Jesus." The second was to point out that passion is needed to do it: "The stronger the love, or the stronger the hate, the more life-like is the figure which is produced." [26] It is not the dispassionate study of the scholar that helps us to know Jesus but the passionate creativity of the artist.

If we are to know Jesus, we need to have this creative

interest in drawing his picture according to our own understanding. The important point is not whether it agrees with other people's but whether it is our own. This is part of what is involved in getting to know Jesus, and an unavoidable part. It is something that we have to do, each in his own way.

It must be each in his own way, for knowing is a personal activity and knowing a person is doubly so. I can know him only as I see him, not as others see him. If a group of us have a common friend whom we all know well, each of us will talk about him in a different way and draw a different picture of him, yet he is the one man and our different pictures of him may all be true. Once we move into the world of knowing people, we have come into a free world where nothing is imposed on us. This is one of the risks we run in making knowing Jesus and not the acceptance of a creed the basis of our Christian faith. Freedom is what we find in Jesus and we must not refuse it, but it commits us to the task of getting to know him each in his own way, as an artist does.

Through the changing of our attitudes

The joy of coming to know someone makes us see life in a new light. Coming to know Jesus has inevitably the same effect. We begin painfully changing our attitudes, our way of looking at people and things. We see from the Gospels how hard it was for the first disciples to abandon familiar conventions and inherited attitudes, and they had the inestimable privilege of observing firsthand how he saw things and treated people. It took a long time for them to see life afresh with their own eyes. He had to awaken their imaginations and shock them into seeing. This was the point of his parables and the point, too, of many of the things that he did. As they began less to question and more to wonder at what Jesus was doing, they began to see other people with more sympathy. And as they exercised their imagination on others, they began to know themselves better, and they found that they were getting to know Jesus, what manner of man he was.

The changing of our attitudes is the third stage in getting to know Jesus. It is not so much a change in our attitude toward him as a change in our attitude toward other people, to life, to the situation we are in, to ourselves. It is, as with the disciples, inspired by our uncomfortable vision of Jesus. It is our inherited attitudes that we find challenged. We realize that it is only as we step into the future that we begin to see other people afresh and can know Jesus at all. We begin to look at life and the world, other people and ourselves, with an imagination awakened to wonder and pain. It is all part of the way by which we learn to know life and ourselves and Jesus.

The close connection between our political and social attitudes and our knowledge of Jesus can perhaps best be exemplified by a particular case. The story of Dietrich Bonhoeffer is that of a man who, beginning with a very conventionally theological view of the Christian faith, came to see Jesus in a new light and to interpret the meaning of being a Christian in a revolu-

tionary way. The change came about through Hitler's
rise to power in Germany and Bonhoeffer's involvement
in political opposition. He had to give up looking at
Jesus from inherited religious attitudes because he saw
his country's political situation with eyes that had been
opened. As he wrote from prison: "The Christian is not
a 'homo religiosus,' but man, pure and simple, just as
Jesus was man, compared with John the Baptist any-
how." [27] It is almost certain that there would have been
for Bonhoeffer no new theological insights without the
painful appreciation of a new political situation and of
his duty to act in it. On the other hand, without the
urge to see Jesus afresh with his own eyes, it is doubtful
that he would have been so concerned with the political
situation. Changing of attitudes and a new knowledge of
Jesus went together.

He had come to feel that the accepted religious life of
the church in Germany and its theology did not reflect
the Jesus whom he was coming to know. As his friend
and biographer, Eberhard Bethge, writes: "Bonhoeffer
regards the characteristics of religion we have mentioned as failing to recognize not only the presence but
also the person of Jesus. The basic thing is always
[Jesus] and the way he is present to us." [28] He goes on
to explain how this new way of seeing Jesus differed
from the old: "(1) Jesus does not call for any acceptance of preliminary systems of thought and behaviour;
(2) he is anti-individual, and, in a totally exposed and
unprotected way, the man for others; (3) he does not
pray as if he had made part payment by instalments,
but with his life; (4) he turns away from the tempta-

tion of the *deus ex machina;* (5) he turns away from the privileged classes and sits down with the outcasts; and (6) he liberates men to find their responsible answer to life through his own powerlessness, which is both shaming and utterly convincing." [29]

Bonhoeffer's words about Jesus are simplest in the last years of his life and especially at the very end when death was imminent. They are very different from the tortuous words of his earlier books. They would indicate that it was his political commitment in the strangest of circumstances which led him to the conviction that he knew Jesus and that knowing him was all that mattered. It is often only in a crisis of personal danger that a man says such things, because he is convinced of the truth of them.

Bonhoeffer's picture of Jesus may not conform to any one else's, but it was his own and it was living. It arose out of a changed attitude to life that caused him to discover Jesus afresh. Many other instances could be given of men and women who have come to a new knowledge of Jesus because in the demanding conditions in which they lived and out of the urgent need for action they found themselves looking at their situation, other people, and themselves in a new light.

Acting, art, attitudes—all these are creative responses to the desire to know Jesus through doing something. They are necessary stages in our growing knowledge of him. They are the equivalent of those first responses of contact, curiosity, and companionship which we make in daily life in meeting someone we want to get to know. In the case of someone whom we cannot meet in the flesh, it is not enough merely to know a multitude of facts about him. These activities of acting, art, and the changing of attitudes, however superficial they may at times seem to be, are gestures of intention and commitment. They are the first teetering steps into the future, into action, into knowing more fully the person who has inspired them.

Through action

Acting, art, changing of attitudes—these are all first steps. They are preludes to action. There remains action itself, and it is through action that we get to know Jesus properly, if we ever do.

Action is different from the other three. In them there is always a vicarious element. In playacting we are thinking ourselves into the life of another person. In a very superficial way we do this even in the wearing of a badge. In a very profound way we do it when we worship. Art, at least representational art, is the expression of our understanding of another person. And when we find that we are altering our attitudes, it is because of new enlightenment that has come to us through someone else or through some event. But an action, in its purity, has nothing vicarious about it. It is something I do on my own. It is essentially personal. The creation of the artist or the discovery of the scientist is the perfect type of action. "The inspired acts of creation seem to occur after a person has struggled hard to discover a new truth, a new idea, or the solution to some vexing and pressing problem. . . . They arise in the mind of their creator spontaneously, effortlessly, and sometimes playfully." [30] These creative acts of the artist and the scientist may seem far removed from the simple things that most of us do, but they are the models for the significant actions by which we grow into knowledge of Jesus. Of course, he is our example. Of course, we try to obey his teaching. Of course, we do things in imitation of him or in obedience to him, and we learn much from these deliberate attempts. These, our efforts to imitate and obey, are our equivalent of the hard struggles of the artist and the scientist before he finds his moment of creation. But these in themselves are not creative actions. They are not really our actions. Our own actions are what we do "spontaneously, effortlessly, and sometimes playfully."

It is when we enter this realm of freedom of action that we begin to know Jesus, for we have come into his world. This is why we can never make up a list of the actions that Christians should take. Once we make such a list, the actions to be taken cease to be my actions. They become the program of some group or party or church. We need, of course, these programs of action in church and society, and we need to give much more thought to them. But we have to see them for what they are—lines of political, social, and ecclesiastical policy, not particularly ways in which we learn to know Jesus. I venture into knowing him in the things I do that are creative, my own, of my own free will, spontaneous, to the glory of God. Such actions, rare as they are, can be corporate but they must be personal. Indeed, there must always be this corporate character in them, for they are done in relation with other people. Because they are personal, they can never be tabulated or imposed on others as a program. It is even dangerous to give examples!

Few will deny that this quality of spontaneous creativity is somewhat lacking among Christians today. Perhaps this is because we so discourage it. It's the quality we so much admire in many of those we regard as our heroes and saints. We see it almost outrageously in Francis of Assisi. We see it in men who do outstandingly dangerous things just for the joy of doing them. We see it in unknown people who give themselves in love to others. They are not concerned about purpose or result. What they do they do for its own sake, to the glory of God. We don't get to know Jesus fully unless we learn to exercise something of this quality, the quality we see supremely in him.

The action that one person may feel called to do will seem quite incomprehensible to another. Bonhoeffer, with his new vision of Jesus, decided that he had to take part in a plot to assassinate Hitler. Have we any right to say he was wrong even though we cannot see ourselves doing it? We are not discussing how we think people ought to act. We are trying to see how we learn to know Jesus through the freedom of acting spontaneously. We learn only when we are free to choose for ourselves and are free to make mistakes.

Freedom and the knowledge of freedom, choice and the spontaneous certainty that seems to eliminate choice, and the near certainty of being wrong are the conditions that allow us to learn from the things that we do. We can, I suppose, learn from the miraculous success of something we have managed to achieve, but we learn more from our failures, from dissatisfaction with what we have done, and from the need to go on. Was an artist ever completely satisfied with his work? Does a scientist ever feel that there is nothing left to discover? Play is never finished though work may be ended. It may seem strange to say that failure helps us to know Jesus better. When we get to know Jesus, don't we discover someone to whom success or failure seemed not to mean very much, who found the meaning of life in the love of men and the glory of God? We see in him one who was content with the validity of his own actions, and when we say that, we are saying something about life and the world. The freedom of Jesus reveals life's own validity.

By our own actions and by their inadequacy and failure we discover in Jesus the meaning of our life. He is, as Paul says, "the firstborn of every creature." He is "the hope of glory" in men and for men. We see our failures but we also know hope. Our actions help us to know him. We are brought into his life.

Our knowledge of Jesus depends on our personal actions. We can't know him by waiting for him to call. But, though we have talked in this chapter as though such action was an individual thing, we have to be reminded that knowledge and action are always basically corporate things. We cannot know Jesus without other people.

CHAPTER

5

WITH OTHERS

We don't know anyone in isolation

Often we seem to think that knowing someone is an individual affair. Because knowing is a personal activity, we think that it concerns no one else. We assume that all that matters is my attitude to the one I want to know, having nothing to do with other people and very little to do with him. We saw how McTaggart excluded the idea of God from the business of knowing someone. He saw any outside interest as a threat to the friendship that he regarded as the only real thing in the world. We might not think of excluding—or of including —God, but often we would be prepared to exclude everything else. For we tend to see this business of knowing someone as an essentially individual affair.

In the world of thought that we have inherited, this is perhaps inevitable. Despite our current interest in sociology the starting point of our philosophical and theological thinking is still the individual. As John Mac-Murray says: "Modern philosophy is characteristically egocentric. I mean no more than this: that, firstly, it takes the self as the starting-point and not God, or the world or the community; and, secondly, the Self is an individual in isolation, an ego or 'I,' never a 'Thou.'"[31] Theological and religious thinking has even more emphatically had the same starting point. This may well be the reason that so many people today find many philosophers and theologians unhelpful. They seem to be discussing in unintelligible language ideas that mean little to men and women. In ordinary life we do not know this isolated individual from which they start. We know about things only in their setting with other things and in our use of them. We know people with other people and through other people—in community, never in isolation.

I cannot know anyone in his isolation, and I am not in my isolation as I get to know him. In fact, the isolated individual is an abstraction, a specimen that no one has ever seen. I do not know myself in isolation, however isolated I may sometimes feel myself to be. For I feel isolated only in relation to other people. When I find someone, my isolation, whatever it is, breaks down, and in finding someone else I begin to find myself. As Sidney Jourard says: "No man can come to know himself except as an outcome of disclosing himself to another person. . . . Disclosure of man to man appears to be the most direct means by which we all learn wherein we are identical with our fellow man and where we differ."[32] But even to talk as if before we met we were both isolated is wrong. There are always others around us. Even this face-to-face meeting of "I" and "Thou" depends on our relationship with many other

people. We could not know anybody, least of all ourselves, except through them.

Learning through others

Our ability to know other people—and, indeed, our
awareness that there are other people—is a skill we
learn as infants and continue to develop all our life. A
child does not have to find his mother, but he has to
discover her as a person, and this discovery is the beginning of his conscious life as a human being. "A person
makes his appearance by entering into relation with
other persons." [33] In discovering his mother a child begins to discover himself as a person. Then he finds that
there are other persons. He begins to distinguish between them as distinct persons. How does he learn to
do this? Presumably he does it by noticing that they
are sometimes together and sometimes separate and by
observing that they make different sounds and do different things and treat him in different ways. He comes
to realize that his environment, which is his family,
is made up of a number of different people. He also
comes slowly to realize that there are other people outside and that they also impinge on his life. The realization that he lives in a world of unknown other people
can come as a shock or as an excitement. He may resent
the fact that he is not the center of his mother's world.
The world of other people can also strike a child with
the fascination of mysterious terror. Osbert Sitwell tells
in his autobiography, *Left Hand, Right Hand,* how the
first words he learned as a child were "rags" and

"bones" from hearing the cry each early morning under his nursery window in Scarborough, with its terrifying intimation that life was not so comfortable or secure outside as it was within. This realization that there are other people whom he does not know often comes to a child earlier than we think and in unexpected ways. Whom he sees and the way they are introduced to him by those whom he trusts determine the beginning of his knowledge of the world of other people, whether it is a world of resentment, curiosity, or dread.

This process does not end in infancy. It goes on and on and never ends. We depend on others, even on strangers, to interpret the world to us. We depend on others for our knowledge of our most intimate friends. This is seen in the way in which many a son gets to know his father. A child has to learn to know his parents. This knowledge is not given to him. In his first years he begins to know his mother without difficulty. Whether he knows his father as intimately depends on how much he sees of him and in what circumstances. When the father leaves home early in the morning to go to work and comes back late in the afternoon with other things still to do, he can become a rather remote person to his children. The danger for the child is that he sees his father as a functionary and not as a person, just as with his mother the danger is that he does not advance from the stage of infantile dependence. His knowledge of his parents, and especially of his father, has to grow by the help of other people. When the father works with the home as his base, the child sees his father in contact with other people. There are still a diminishing number of such cases—the farmer with his staff, the doctor with his patients, the clergyman with his parishioners, the village shopkeeper with his customers. Through his attitude toward them and their attitude toward him the child learns more about his father than through his own personal contacts. And he learns things about his father that he cannot easily learn otherwise. He sees him in working contacts with other adults. The child needs to see his parents through the eyes of those with whom they work and play in order to get to know them. Knowledge based solely on the parent-child relationship can be very inadequate. It can be too self-conscious to be mutually revealing. The child learns to know his father not so much from what his father says to him as from what he overhears his father saying to other people and other people saying to him. We have to learn to know people, just as we have to learn to talk and walk. Indeed, it is part of speech and action.

Our knowledge of those closest to us, such as our parents, brothers, sisters, and our more intimate family friends, depends on their relationships with other people. It is with their help that we see them in the round and realize, sometimes to our pain, that they do not exist solely for us. These others who help us are not confined to the people we meet. Their parents and grandparents, their old friends and their heroes, also help us in our understanding of them, for they helped to set the patterns of their lives. They also help us to understand ourselves, for this was the pattern of life into which we were born.

Learning through the community

We know people in their relationships. We know them through the other people they know and who know them. Knowing someone is never merely a mutual business of "I and Thou." It involves more than individuals. It involves the community in which men are set. Knowing a person is not a constant, unchanging activity to which all cases conform. Doubtless there was a basic uniformity in the way in which David knew Jonathan and Socrates knew Plato and Peter knew Jesus and Boswell knew Johnson. But each person brings a different pattern of relationships, a different experience of other people, and a different background of living. These are formed by the community in which he lives, by his acceptance or rejection of it. Knowing someone in a small, rural community is different from knowing someone in a highly concentrated, industrial setting or in a sophisticated, intellectual society. It is always contemporary and it is always demanding. We can know people only in our own and their own situation.

Our situation is never easier to understand than it is to understand ourselves. It is so difficult to understand that we are often tempted to think that it would be much easier to know people if we lived in a simpler society. We have a happy picture of the medieval village or the English rural parish of the eighteenth century or the nineteenth-century small town in New England. We think of them as compact little societies in which everyone knew everyone else and all were bound together in conscious, intimate relationships. There is no way to test the truth of this ideal picture. What we can say with some confidence is that in these little societies everyone knew the place and function of everyone else in the community and that these were unchanging. You knew what use, if any, you could make of other people and what demands they could make on you. The fact that people were often known by their functions, as the miller, the postman, etc., is an indication that people were thought of as functionaries rather than as persons.

It is difficult for us now to imagine what life was like in these little, self-contained communities. Ronald Blythe's delectable book *Akenfield: Portrait of an English Village* studies the emergence of such a community into our present world and in so doing helps us to see that old world better. It gives an intimate and sympathetic description of the inhabitants of a Suffolk village of the present day. We see the old village at the beginning of this century coming with difficulty but not with reluctance into the life of the modern world. In the old village what marked one man off from the others and gave him dignity was his work, but it was not a means of a man's knowing his neighbors. Work made each man unique and kept him isolated. Ronald Blythe emphasizes that a man's knowledge of his work was incommunicable. A veil of secrecy covered the village, and this was over the homes of the people too. "Who really knows about the cottages?" he asks. "They are still mysterious. Much of the life in them is still concealed." [34] He refers to a man's home village as being also his prison, and he shows how industry in the adjacent town, or the call of the sea, or war brought to men a new and welcome knowledge of the life of the world, an understanding of other people, and an opening up of life for them. In contrast to those who had, by breaking away, found new life in wider relationships, he points to "the sometimes crushing, limiting power which the village exerts on families which have never escaped." [35]

This study leaves us with a glimpse of the grimmer side of life of the early village, from which there was no escape. No doubt there were in it the possibilities of deep mutual understanding, but there is also little doubt that any young man who wanted to do anything somehow had to get away. And when the winds of social change began to blow, the call was imperative. Jesus had to break away from Nazareth and his home, and he made his disciples do the same. The shaking of social conventions seems necessary if we are to get to know one another and extend the range of those we know. A static, small society can be destructive of creativity. Our world must always be a changing world.

An example from another country may be helpful:

China for centuries, until the present revolution, had known a rigid social pattern based on clearly defined relationships. These, according to Confucian teaching, were those of ruler and subject, father and son, husband and wife, elder brother and younger, friend and friend. No one in the old days came to know Chinese society however slightly but felt the strength of the hold this pattern had on all the people. At the same time he was uncomfortably aware of a certain impersonality in social life. The wisdom of "saving face" prevented open conflict, but it also prevented openness of opinion and growth in personal relationships. It was also impossible to see people of the present day confined in these Confucian relationships. They seemed inadequate for the world into which China was moving. There was nothing in them about the relationship of employer and employee, neighbor and neighbor, rich and poor. Chinese students who went abroad and in European and American colleges became accustomed to a different pattern of relationships found great difficulty on their return to China in fitting into the old fixed pattern of domestic and social relationships. They complained that the old life was too impersonal.

Today we in the West, in contradistinction to those in the developing countries of the East and the South, seem to have turned things round. We complain that our modern world is impersonal. We pine for the village, the corner shop, the little group of people of whom we can make use. We think we would really get to know people there. What we are really doing is to run away from knowing people in our own world. We have equated a personal world with a cozy world. We have no right to do so. The small community can be an impersonal community. It sometimes has to be to survive. The world we live in is huge, and it is changing but it is not impersonal. What is frightening is that we share it with so very many people, many of whom fulfill functions we do not understand and whose circumstances we find it hard to appreciate. But we know about them. We know that for our survival and our comfort we depend on the labor and permit the poverty of millions whom we have never seen. We know that our actions may bring starvation or destruction to others. We don't and can't know all the people with whom we are bound up in the bundle of life, but we know that they exist. We know something of how they just exist. We are aware that our common future depends on more than just knowing about them, that somehow we have to learn to know one another. But we cannot know anyone apart from this world in which we live—even Jesus!

We can't know Jesus in isolation

If we have imagined that we can know a friend in isolation, how much more have we taken it for granted that we can know Jesus in isolation? We seem to think that the only way we can know Jesus is in the privacy of some uniquely personal experience. Getting to know Jesus has been regarded as a confrontation that the individual must face by himself. He may be invited to the confrontation in a crowd and in all the blaze of publicity, but what he is asked to do is to make an individual act of decision and enter into a personal relationship with Jesus. This is not the way we can get to know Jesus or anyone else. In fact, it is almost certain to prevent such a thing from happening. The only way in which we can see someone in isolation is by regarding him as a ruler or a judge or a leader or a television star or even as a teacher. His isolated authority depends on our not getting to know him. We may react to him with admiration or obedience or fear. But we do not know him.

How we get to know Jesus

We know someone only if he gives to us a sense of freedom, of purpose, and of unity. We can see him as a liberator because we see him in his relationship to other people. The only way in which we can come to know Jesus now is by seeing him in his relationship to other people. By what he did and what he said Jesus made this explicit in three ways.

First, he chose to live his life as much with other people as possible. On rare occasions he went off by himself for rest and quiet. Otherwise he lived as publicly as he could in all the turmoil of a disintegrating society. We see in the Gospels an old society desperately clinging to a rigid pattern of individual function and social behavior: The foreigner must keep himself and his money out of the Temple. Men must not work on the Sabbath even to help people. The Pharisees had all the answers. The high priest would tell the nation what to do. The carpenter's son must not ape the scribe. But the system was breaking down. Whenever the people vehemently defended it, Jesus disregarded it. He did not treat people according to their accepted functions as prophet, priest, or king. He dealt with people in their personal relationships and talked of their productive capacities as fishermen, farmers, and merchants. If we think we have been born into an unfortunate period of the world's history now, Jesus could far more strongly have protested against the time and place of his birth. Yet it was at such a time that he claimed that men must know and love one another. He made no exceptions; he said that this was the same as knowing and loving God.

He was prepared to meet and deal with people all together. He welcomed the individuals who came to him, but he went out to meet the crowd. The one thing he seemed never to allow was that someone should draw him away to be alone with him. If people wanted to meet him, they had to meet all sorts of other people as well. Individual contact with him was never enough. He dealt with people just as they were, in the mass, by the side of the lake, on the road to Jerusalem, in the Temple. His contact with them, however, was not impersonal because he dealt with them in the mass. It was in this difficult setting that he brought men to know one another and so to know him. He spoke about the Kingdom of God, but the words he used were about ordinary people doing ordinary things with other ordinary people. He was talking about life and, therefore, about people.

Second, when he chose his twelve men to be the political group through whom he would work, he made them live a corporate life. He made them break loose from the set pattern of village and family life, but not by being a cozy, little group on their own. They had to come to know him in a deeper way but they could do this only by coming to know one another in a deeper way. This demand to live together and work together was what they found hard in following Jesus. He forced them into wider contacts by making them meet all kinds of people in all manner of situations. Whenever they wanted to escape from others, he made them stay with them and see them in a new light. When they wanted to send the mothers and their children away, he took a child and said that this was the person they should follow. When they wanted him to send the crowd away so that they could enjoy a spiritual retreat, he made them feed the people. He attacked their love of isolation from all sides. They wanted to remain isolated from foreigners, strangers, women, children, outcasts. Their love of isolation had become for them a virtue. It had been built up by their education, their religious customs, their national pride. He led them into the world of other men, of all other men. For them isolation was at an end. And, in the ending of isolation, they began really to know Jesus.

Third, Jesus had his own distinctive teaching about the whole business of knowing. When he talked about knowing, he always spoke in the plural. He never said, "Thou knowest" or "One of you knows" or "Some of you will know." It was always, "You know," "You know together." He never suggested that one of them knew more than the others or would ever know more than the others. He made this strikingly clear when he said that they already knew the secrets of the Kingdom of God. Quite obviously they didn't think they did. They were always waiting for Jesus to reveal his secret to them. They thought of a secret as some arcane mystery, some important message they could either whisper in someone's ear or withhold, something they would know and other people would not know. When Jesus talked about the secrets of the Kingdom, he was not thinking of this kind of factual information that can be passed by word of mouth and can be the subject of examination or of inquiry. The secrets were the lessons that they had learned in their life together, and they could know them only corporately, not individually. There is nothing strange in this—it is part of our common experience. There are things that a close-knit family knows corporately. This knowledge is quite different from the sum of the factual knowledge of all its members. It is expressed in its style of life, its way of looking at things, its way of acting in a crisis. In a nation at times of danger or crisis there are things that we all know together and that we do not question. And in the church there are things that we know together which are greater than the things we know and believe as individuals. This we express in our worship. Of course, the family may be corporately selfish and the nation blind to the needs of others and the church limited in its worship, but this does not disprove the strength and the reality of this corporate knowledge. It is when we can dare to say "We know" that we are in the realm of what Jesus was talking about. It is the realm in which we have knowledge of people. Fortunately we talk about it with difficulty. We can really express it only in action or in worship.

Help from Martin Buber

The practices and teachings of Jesus help us to understand how we come to know other people. They certainly point to the way we know him today. What he revealed about corporate knowing we take for granted in certain limited areas of life. It is probable that before this age with its emphasis on the self men took this corporate knowledge for granted in much broader areas. A child begins his thinking life by talking in terms of "we." He identifies himself with the other people who make up his life. In youth he discovers his identity. He wants to say "I" in self-assertion, protest, or rebellion. Then when he grows into maturity he recognizes a conscious, creative unity with others and uses "we" with a new understanding.

There is the same kind of development in the social thinking of a society or nation. We may be said to be at the stage now when the protest of the individual is over, and we begin to find more enlightenment in our corporate experiences.

Our understanding of the nature of personal knowledge owes a great deal to the work of Martin Buber in this century. His historic book *I and Thou,* published in Germany as long ago as 1913, helped men to see the importance of face-to-face meeting of two persons as the basic means of understanding life in all its richness and mystery. What Buber was emphasizing was not the individual but the personal—the recognition of the other person and, through him, of the "otherness" of life. He was emphasizing the personal as over against the material—"I" and "Thou" as against "it." He was pointing out that the important factor in our knowledge is our recognition of the Other—the other person, the otherness of life, and so of God; knowledge through distinction and relation.

For Buber this knowledge went deeper than meeting people. In a later book Buber described how as a boy he had experienced this personal recognition of the Other in a way that had nothing to do with another person at all. "When I was eleven years of age, spending the summer on my grandparents' estate, I used, as often as I could do it unobserved, to steal into the stable and gently stroke the neck of my darling, a broad dapplegrey horse. It was not a casual delight but a great, certainly friendly, but also deeply stirring happening. If I am to explain it now, beginning from the still very fresh memory of my hand, I must say that what I experienced in touch with the animal was the Other, the immense otherness of the Other, which, however, did not remain strange like the otherness of the ox and the ram, but rather let me draw near and touch it. When I stroked the mighty mane, sometimes marvellously smoothcombed, at other times just as astonishingly wild, and felt the life beneath my hand, it was as though the element of vitality itself bordered on my skin, something that was not I, was certainly not akin to me, palpably the other, not just another, really the Other itself; and yet it let me approach, confided itself to me, placed itself elementally in the relation of *Thou* and *Thou* with me." [36]

Buber was concerned always with the problem and the joy and excitement of knowing. He saw it as founded on the recognition and experience of the Other as the meaning and truth of things. We recognize the other as being related to us and yet quite distinct. He discussed how we *know*. He also discussed how *we* know. Perhaps the title of his best-known book gives the impression that he was concerned with the individual. "I" and

"Thou" are singular pronouns. But he is even more interested in "you" and "we." In a passage in which he emphasized the importance of speech in the business of knowing, Buber had this to say about the "we": "Speech . . . was at all times present whenever men regarded one another in the mutuality of I and Thou; whenever one showed the other something in the world in such a way that from then on he began really to perceive it; whenever one gave another a sign in such a way that he could recognise the designated situation as he had not been able to before; whenever one communicated to the other his own experience in such a way that it penetrated the other's circle of experience and supplemented it from within, so that from now on his perceptions were set within a world as they had not been before. All this flowing again into a great stream of reciprocal sharing of knowledge—thus came to be and thus is the living *WE*, the genuine *WE*, which, where it fulfils itself, embraces the dead who once took part in colloquy and now take part in it through what they have handed down to posterity." [37]

Knowledge is founded on communication—by sign and speech, in meeting, through work and play. There would be no knowledge if we did not know other people in the present and in the past. Knowledge of others is the beginning of knowledge. It is also its crown.

We know Jesus with our contemporaries

We cannot talk about knowing Jesus without the help of innumerable other people, mostly unknown and mostly dead. We can't talk about knowing him without sharing the baffling life of the innumerable people who make up the situation in which we live today. Knowing people is a matter of sharing a common situation that we may not like and against which we may rebel. When conditions are acceptable to us we conform to convention and so absolve ourselves from thinking. We see people as the fulfillers of certain functions and so do not need to treat them as persons. When men have rebelled against accepted conventions and broken loose from rigid patterns of behavior and have tried to find or to get back to a more intelligible way of life, they have begun to discover other people, or at least some other people, and so to discover themselves. It is then that they start new groups and societies and make experiments in social living. The early monastic movement offers many examples. Francis of Assisi and the society he founded give a conspicuous example. They all arose out of social turmoil and acute dissatisfaction with the accepted pattern of life, and they all aroused the suspicion of the conventional. There are plenty of examples in the present day. New groups act in the name of Jesus and claim to have come to know him. They see him as a man like themselves and yet different. So they have to change their way of life. They belong to their generation and protest against it. For protest is a sign of belonging. And now we see that their generation belongs to them.

Today we are certainly trying to know ourselves and other men. We realize that we must do so if the world is to survive. We may think that it is our institutions which we are trying to understand but it is really ourselves. What we are continually discussing is really our relationship one to another as men and women, old and young, East and West, North and South. We don't know what kind of people we are but we want to know. We are looking for the picture of authentic man in our society.

Perhaps we should consider ourselves fortunate that we in this age cannot escape from involvement with others, with the innumerable people with whom we live in our immediate communities, and with the millions more on whom we depend. We can, perhaps better than our fathers or grandfathers, appreciate the tension of the society in which Jesus lived—its hopes and fears. He speaks to our condition, as he spoke to theirs, not by offering escape from it but by showing that sharing and suffering and hope are inescapable. The point of all his teaching and actions is the eternal importance of mutual personal relationships; in other words, of love. This is far more central to his life and teaching than all the functions and titles that his followers and critics have tried to fasten on him. It was for this that he suffered in the end.

He sees no difference between the attitude of men to their fellowmen and their attitude to himself. It is not so much that they must know their fellows in order to know him, as if the one were the training for the other. It is, rather, that in knowing their fellowmen they know him—there is no difference. It is their attitude to "the least of these my brethren" that indicates whether they know their fellowmen. What mattered was how they treated the least of their fellows. He took a child as his example of the least. We are apt to think that it was of a child's innocence that he spoke when he claimed that of such is the Kingdom of Heaven. It was not a child's innocence but the fact that children were utterly disregarded that made him make the claim. This was obvious from those others whom he set before them— the publicans and the prostitutes. They saw him welcome and treat as his equals those whom others did all in their power to avoid meeting at all. They were of the Kingdom of God simply because they were men and women. It was useless for men to talk about knowing him unless they knew the least of their fellows. It was pointless, for if they did not want to know them, they would not want to know him.

Men have always found this very difficult to accept. All through the church's history there have been those who in his name have gone out to serve the sick, the unfortunate, and the depraved. They have been trying to follow him but not wholly to share his life. In taking his name they have identified themselves with his actions. They have been doing what they think he would want them to do. They have healed the sick in his name. They have preached the gospel in his name. In a sense they have been trying to act like Jesus to people in distress, but this is not what Jesus meant. They were not to be Jesus to other men—they were to see Jesus in other men. It is almost impossible for most of us to get near this, but to realize our failure is our first step to

knowing Jesus. We begin to know him when we realize
that we can't know him apart from others and especially those who are thought the least. We can't know
anyone unless we belong to the company he keeps. We
can't know Jesus without being involved with other men.
This awareness that he belongs to all other men and
very particularly to the unfortunate has been the reason
why in every age men have known him as a contemporary who spoke to their condition. In every age, but
especially in times of uncertainty and revolution, other
men and particularly those who are suffering have been
those with whom their fellows have had to make contact. Their demands have been inescapable.

Our attitude toward other men depends on the kind
of picture we have of them, and this depends not so
much on our information about them as on our picture
of the man we are most glad to know and are trying to
know better. This man can never be just the ideal of a
man, for we can never know the ideal, and the thought
of it condemns us and brings disillusionment. It can
only be a real man, a particular man who lived and
died and yet is man. Such a one we can know, and only
such a one can we know.

The mystery of our knowing Jesus lies in his universal
human identity. He is not the ideal of what men should
be. He is not a moral example or rebuke. He is essential
man and thus known in every man. We know other men
through Jesus and we know Jesus through other men.
Is this what Paul meant when he called Jesus "the firstborn of every creature"? He was saying something about
every man just as much as he was saying something

about Jesus. We cannot know a contemporary friend unless we share the company he keeps. We cannot know Jesus unless somehow we share his universal company.

And is not this where we can claim that there is that mutual response which is the sign of "knowledge of" as distinct from "knowledge about"? In face-to-face contact with a contemporary friend there is mutual response. I respond to him and he responds to me. In the case of someone in the past whom I admire and study and even love, I respond to him. I may find a new direction to my life through knowing about him. I may well change my attitudes and opinions. I can see how Sandburg responded to Lincoln and can imagine how Gibbon responded to Homer. It is real but it is one-way. The response I find coming from other people is different from the response I make. I am in no way responsible for it. Maslow hints that he knew something like this through his affection for and engagement in the continuing work of his chosen philosophers of the past. There is more than a hint of this in the experience of the response that Jesus makes to us through other men, through those who claim to know him but also through those who make no such claim—the least of these his brothers.

The church

And this is where the church comes in. It is not in the church that we know Jesus, but in the world. We know him in the life of love, suffering, and hope that he shares with all men. But without the church few of us would be in the position to recognize him in the world.

The church exists because of Jesus. It exists because some men had come to know him and were convinced that he belonged to all other men and that they should come to know him. This knowing of Jesus is the prime origin and hidden being of the church. This does not mean that the church is always aware of its origin or of its hidden being any more than any of us constantly realize that the basis and meaning of our daily life depend on our knowledge of other people and their knowledge of us. We find other things to do that take up our time, and the church has found other things to do that seem all-demanding. Perhaps Jesus told his first disciples so fully about his own temptations because he knew that these same temptations would confront them when they had work to do and choices to make and power to wield. They would be tempted to win support by the obvious value of their work. They would be tempted to exercise power over men for their own good. They would be tempted to tell men what they must believe and to impose belief by any means. All these things, which can be called good in themselves, can be done without knowing Jesus at all. Indeed, knowing him may raise doubts and questions and rebellion. These temptations are inevitable for those who take their work and themselves seriously. We must always remember that Jesus knew them and resisted them. And knowing Jesus means that we know why. For we have learned what freedom means.

Without the church it is hard to see how we would know him and for three reasons:

First, it is the church that has preserved the basic facts about Jesus on which our knowledge of him must be based. It has preserved the New Testament not as a priceless ancient document to be kept safe in a museum nor as a holy relic. It has preserved it as a book to be read and, therefore, to be copied, translated, and circulated. It has made the public reading of it, and especially of the four Gospels, the foundation of its worship. It would be impossible to estimate the effect of the public reading of the facts of Jesus' life Sunday by Sunday down the centuries on the memory and imagination of people. In the ages when only the clergy were literate, the power of the heard word was, of course, greater than it is today, but at all times the repetition of familiar stories has had great educational power. We know this with children. But it has its power also with the literate and sophisticated, as we know from drama, television, radio, and worship. We would now regard books as the means by which we know about Jesus, but without the worship of the church, knowledge might not have been preserved until the advent of printing. Still, corporate hearing provides something that solitary reading cannot give.

This continuous, habitual, and almost mechanical re-iteration of what Jesus did and said did not survive for its own sake. And this brings us to the second reason: the church is made up of the people who are linked together by this story. It is the succession of all kinds of people who down the centuries have asked their questions or seen their visions and tried to work out what this hearing about Jesus meant—or who just listened. What they

heard they related to their own lives and to life around
them, not to the life he had lived in unknown Palestine.
This succession of people united in the name of Jesus is
the only true apostolic succession, much more valid than
any tradition of ordination or continuity of belief. Buildings last for a long time, but in the end they fall down.
Dogmas last as long, but words change their meaning.
The only lasting continuity is the continuity of persons,
all different but with something in common. The church
has provided this continuity in life through men's ever-
changing knowledge of Jesus. This is quite different
from the narrow continuity offered in books to scholars.
It is the continuity of varied experience in widely different circumstances of people with divergent questions
and varied needs. It is the continuity of a family or a
community or a nation, but the continuity of the church
goes back much farther than any of these and includes
a vastly wider range of people. This is why it is so difficult for us to escape from knowing Jesus now. Knowledge of him is not a merely literary knowledge. It lives
among people.

There is a third way in which the church helps us, or
should help us, to grow into the knowledge of Jesus. The
church in whatever unit it gathers men and women together for worship provides in microcosm the same net-
work of personal relationships that men face in greater
complexity in the wider world. Whatever be the size of
the congregation or group in which he worships, a member of the church is in contact with other persons. He
may not want to have anything to do with them. Together they may not be at all clear as to what they
should be doing. They may all, if asked, assert that

their faith is an individual thing. But for all that, they are a company, tied to one another by all sorts of contacts of acquaintance, friendship, suspicion, dislike, or fear, with the added discomfort of a faith that demands another kind of life. They are also, although they often forget it, connected to one another by all the outside ties of employment, service, trade, or neighborhood which bind everyone in the community together. Their life in the local church is the microcosm of the life of the world outside, with this difference: they are aware of their life together and are aware that they must deal with it somehow. They may deal with it by disregarding it and making their church their citadel of individual isolation from the world and from one another. Or they may together turn in on themselves and build up a cozy little life of their own. Or they may recognize that they have been given the opportunity of learning how to live together in the world today. It is only as the church follows this last line that it could dare to take to itself Benedict's definition of his monastery as "a school in the Lord's service." It would then be a place where we are deliberately trying to find out what life with Jesus means, what his teachings mean, how we are to understand the situation in which we are, how we are to live with all other men. It involves the breaking down of the barriers of reticence and convention among members. It means getting to know people as they are. This is the essential help that the church should give us in our getting to know Jesus better. The continuity of the church should enable each generation to come to know him in its own way.

Whether the local church is such a school is another

question, but however much it fails, it is unquestionably a cross section of contemporary society, facing the issues of modern life and being uncomfortably impelled to corporate questioning and experimentation by a common faith.

The church is the continuous reminder to us that we can never know Jesus by ourselves alone or attain knowledge of him by study in isolation. It certainly would be easier for the church today if it could see its task simply to get things done or to rule benevolently over men or to inspire belief. But the essence of the church is being with people and so knowing Jesus.

Is there any other way of knowing him? Is there any other way in which we can say that he still lives for us? Our knowledge of him is the only test: We know him when he draws us into relationship with other people. We know him when he gives us life and vision and the hope of glory. What more do we ask? It seemed enough for Paul. Is not this to know him and the power of his resurrection and the fellowship of his sufferings?

THE MYSTERY OF KNOWING

There is no doubt that today myriads of people know Jesus, or think they do. They take their knowledge of him for granted just as they take for granted their knowledge of their family and friends. They would never think of questioning either. And this, in the end, is proof that they know him.

Yet it is a matter of wonder that we should know Jesus at all. After so many hundreds of years, with the records of what he did and said written in a form that is foreign to us today and with all the subsequent accumulation of legend, superstition, doubts, and theologizing, it is surely strange that men today are so confident that they know him. Attempts are continually being made to prove that we do not know him at all. There are those who claim that there was no such person or that the picture we have drawn of him does not tally with the few facts of which we can be absolutely certain. These views enjoy sporadic fashion. They are ready subjects for study, research, and debate, but they regularly fade away before men's confident assurance that

Jesus is a person whom they know. We have better means of knowing about him than we have of knowing about almost any other man in the remote past, of whose existence we would never have any doubt. We know more about him than most of us know about our great-grandparents. And of their existence we have never any doubt. We ourselves are the evidence for their past existence. We would not be here if they had not existed. This same line of proof applies to our knowledge of Jesus. The Gospels provide us with the factual foundation for our knowledge about Jesus, but our study of them, necessary as it is, is not really the basis of our knowledge of him. We know him because we as men, and not just as Christians, are of his family. We know him through the experience of men and women of many generations and through our own taste of life. We cannot help knowing him. But the wonder still remains that we do.

But there is a deeper wonder: the wonder that we should want to know him. He does not conform to the image of man that in all ages men have admired. In every age men have adopted their heroes. They have magnified their images. They have erected statues to them and painted their pictures and honored their graves. There have been conquerors who ruled great dominions, as Caesar and Napoleon. There have been teachers who have left impressive memorials in their writing, as Plato and Confucius. There have been men who have founded states, as Washington and Garibaldi. These have been men's heroes and their models of greatness. To this Valhalla of heroes Jesus does not belong. In this picture of famous men he does not have a place. He does not qualify for such company. If he were there at all, he would be found among the spectators or in the crowd outside. Of course, men have tried to assure him a place. They have given him titles and ascribed to him roles that would guarantee him a place. They have pointed to him as a conqueror greater than Napoleon, as a teacher greater than Plato, as the founder of a nation greater than George Washington. They have described him as a warrior fighting a battle with the world. Or they have seen him as a defender of moral standards, or as the final judge of men, or as the supreme example. But these descriptions of the roles men want him to fulfill tell us nothing about him as a person. He slips through them and appears to those who know him as quite a different man. The Jesus whom men know from the records and from their experience and that of other men bears no relation to the picture that men would draw of a possible savior of the world or their ideal or perfect man. Indeed, they see him in two ways that in another they would call repelling. They see him doing what they do not want to see, and they hear him telling them to be what they do not want to be. Yet men want to know him.

We plaster our houses with the sign of the cross in the very structure of our doors and windows. But a cross with a man nailed to it is the last thing most of us would like to look upon. We glibly talk about Jesus as "the suffering servant," forgetting that the first thing we want to avoid is suffering and the last thing we want to be is a servant. We need to take seriously Isaiah's word,

which the church has taken as referring to Jesus, if we
are to get the true meaning of that phrase. "He hath
no form nor comeliness; and when we shall see him,
there is no beauty that we should desire him. He is despised and rejected of men; . . . and we hid as it were
our faces from him." If we want to see him, it is not
because he is the successful man, the mature man, the
perfect man, but because he is like us, like what we are
afraid we are, like what we are afraid to be, just a
man.

If the cross is what no one wants to see, the other side
of it is what no one wants to be. Men saw him during his
life on earth, and men have known him since as one who
is free, uncompromising and yet uncensorious, open to
all, indifferent to men's conventions and assumptions,
observant of beauty, welcoming to children, unresisting.
This is the other side, because it was for this that he
suffered. This is the kind of person we are all afraid of
being, yet this is the man that people want to know.
They see him as made of the same stuff of which they
are made, but they see him making something quite
different of it.

That we should know him is a wonder. That we
should want to is a mystery. That wonder and that
mystery tell us far more about ourselves than about
him. Or perhaps it would be better to say that they
tell us something about the common humanity that we
share with him. They tell us something about the
strange business of being a man. They reveal something
of the root of our joys and fears and hopes, so often
unexpressed. We begin to see where we find the real

meaning of our life—in the vision of beauty and in the glimpse of truth and, above all, in the understanding of love. The abiding mystery is in ourselves, in the incomprehensible, satisfying but unsatisfied nature of life. All the mystery comes down in the end to "knowing." If our glory is that we should know Jesus and find in him the light that flickers in every man, the mystery remains: How do we know him?

The mystery of knowing

What do I mean when I say that I know him? The business of knowing someone is, as David Cairns says, "a dimension which is the privilege of persons alone." [38] We take this privilege for granted. We do not ask what we mean by knowing people any more than we would ask what our life means. But if we want to understand the nature of our human life, then we must try to understand what mutual knowledge of persons means, for this is our life. Animals recognize other animals, and other particular animals, and can have a particular relationship to some. But, so far as we know, only men have the ability of entering into mutual knowledge, which leads into creative activity. This meeting of person with person involves more than mutual recognition and the knowledge of facts about each other. "It contains in it just as important elements of action, will and feeling." [39] By this means we are able to communicate. We can create. We are able to plan for the future. This ability to communicate marks man as different from the rest of creation. On this his ability to think would seem to rest.

Certainly from his ability to communicate with his fellows have developed all his peculiar activities and institutions. We recognize another as a distinct person by appreciating the way he looks and the way he speaks and the things he does and the way he does them. If we were not able to do this, we could only make signs to one another as animals do. We could not converse, for conversation demands both a common language and an individual point of view. Through conversation we are able to exchange thoughts and develop ideas. Without this mutual knowledge of one another, however primitive, there could be no cooperation and therefore no art, no religion, no industry. There could be no trust, no love, no hope.

Knowing someone is what sets us off in the business of living. A child has to come to know his mother in order to begin to live a human life, and this business of learning to know other people continues all through life. Success is not inevitable. It is something we have to learn and to continue to learn all our days. It is not something I do by myself. I need other people all the time. This learning is a corporate affair.

This kind of knowledge is not an examinable subject, but then neither is life. I can never test my knowledge of a person against someone else's knowledge of him. My knowledge is always my own, even as his is his own. And neither is absolute. I cannot ever dare to be dogmatic in my knowledge of a friend, however intimate we may be. He can surprise me by what he says and by what he does. And I expect to be surprised. This unpredictability is part of my knowledge of him.

This mutual knowledge is always of particular persons. It can never be general. It is always personal. It has to do with particular persons, with differing feelings and attitudes and different ways of doing things. Such knowledge is untidy and outwardly inefficient.

So for the sake of efficiency it is claimed that we must "eliminate the personal." Only as we do so will we be confident that things will work out as planned. We base our plans and actions not on knowing people but on dealing with figures. The general plan will be upset if personal considerations are allowed to enter. The manager should not have personal relationships with members of his staff. The officer must live a life different from that of his men. Even the parish minister, according to some, should not make friends in his congregation. It doesn't work. The austere manager becomes a human person when he goes home. His family refuses to believe the stories they hear of his harshness at work. When efficiency breaks down, it is blamed on human weakness and fallibility, but the cause of the trouble is that inhuman efficiency cannot stand up against the human urge to know other people.

So life struggles against the organization of life, and the chance and the pleasure of knowing people get pushed back as a luxury into the private world of home and sport, club and church. All the time we know that the hope of the world depends on our getting to know the innumerable other people with whom we are bound up in the business of living. As our way of life changes and we become involved in mutual dependence on ever-increasing numbers of people, the business of knowing them becomes more necessary, more difficult, and more rewarding.

The way forward is not by regarding as of only private interest the joy of knowing someone as a friend but by building on it as the only sure foundation. It is this personal knowledge that enables me to understand the past and prepare for the future.

Getting to know someone helps me to rejoice in the purpose of life and to see meaning in the past. I know him as one who has done particular things and has had particular experiences, and all these now belong to the past. I cannot know all about them, but the man I know was personally involved in them and was formed by them. His actions explain him. So if I want someone else to know something about him, I don't quote his opinions, for they are bound to be shared by many other people. I describe his actions, for they are his own and particular. In other words, he belongs to the continuum of particular actions that we call history. "Man is a being with a history, and in this history he reveals himself," writes David Cairns. "The story of his history is his own story. Yet he is not just a history, but a being whose mode of existing is historical." [40] The business of knowing other people ties me into their lives and therefore into history. It forces me to take what has happened and is happening in the world seriously. It is the enemy of all generalizations and abstractions. Life is seen as particular people doing particular things. It becomes very untidy. It defies our simplifications and our efficiency, but it has meaning.

And, as we have already seen, knowing a particular person confronts me with an unknown future—his and mine and that of others. And this brings freedom. I am no longer imprisoned in myself. I have been brought into the freedom of life with others, into the freedom of not being my own. I belong now to a world of relationships, for to know someone is a mutual activity. I cannot know without being known. I may think that I know what I am doing when I get to know someone, but I cannot have any idea of what is happening to me when I am known. I am in a world where the unexpected may happen, and this means freedom. This is the risk of love and friendship. The risk is the one thing that gives excitement to the lives of most of us.

Knowing remains a mystery, yet we live by its power. We are kept in life, not by the feasibility of the explanations we give or are given, but by the mystery that stimulates us to find the unexpected and to go on seeking. We cannot explain what this business of knowing one another is any more than we can explain what beauty is or love or life, but we know that if our lives have in them any touch of joy or excitement and any appreciation of truth and beauty, these have come to us through our knowledge of other people. Knowing another person is the first discovery of human life and its final mystery.

The mystery and meaning of knowing Jesus

Knowing depends on the meeting of two people. If I say that I know Jesus, I mean that I, as a particular person, know the particular person who is Jesus. This knowledge is personal and immediate. It is in the first person and in the present time.

I know Jesus, as I know anyone else, when my imagination has been awakened by him and I see life and myself and other people in a new light. This is the proof of my knowing him. And only I can have it. I see him as a particular man who lived in a particular place at a particular time. Unless he is such a person I cannot know him. I see him as one who by the stark simplicity of his life and the fullness of his love was not limited by conditions of time and place but belongs as a man to the life of all men and women and therefore to my life. I see him as living a human life in its simplicity and fullness, and, therefore, his life is of intrinsic significance to my life and the lives of all other people. I find that everything is not explained in him nor every problem solved. That would be the end of life. And life—the mystery of life—is what I find in him. Everything is enlivened by knowing him. In him I find a new wonder at the mystery of life, a new acceptance of love, and a new understanding that life can be lived only in relationship with others and, therefore, I can know the hope of glory.

My imagination may be awakened in many ways. It may be through wonder at his life and at the lives of others. It may be through the awareness of my own failures. It may be through suffering and the understanding it brings. It may come through happenings that have no formal connection with his name. But unless my imagination is awakened by life, I cannot know him, just as I cannot know any friend unless my imagination is somehow stirred by him.

I know Jesus because I find a new freedom through

him. It may be a tantalizing freedom that eludes me because I am afraid to grasp it. It may be a terrifying freedom because I do grasp it and am afraid of the consequences. But this sense of freedom is necessary if I am to know him, as it is indeed if I am to know anyone. For to know someone depends on response, and it is in the mutual response that freedom lies. With a contemporary friend I may easily be possessive in the response I demand and so lose freedom, but with Jesus this is not possible. He belongs, not to me or to my small circle, but to all men. In knowing Jesus we know human life in its mystery, in its simplicity, in its commonness, and in its uniqueness. In him we are given the key to the knowledge of life. In him we have light to see ourselves and others with faith and hope and love. In him we have inherited an unmerited liberty. Knowing Jesus puts the seal on our hesitating conviction that to know someone else is "the only real thing in life."

This knowledge of Jesus comes inevitably only in flashes. This is so with our friends. Our appreciation and understanding of them is not always at a constant pitch. There are moments when something inexplicable happens, and we are lifted into a great light of love and wonder. It is the same with our knowledge of Jesus. There are moments when we are quite certain that we know him. Such moments, different for each one of us, are always in the immediate now, for it is only in the present that I can say "I know."

But the present is only the razor-edge between the past and the future. Personal knowledge of my friends

ties me to the past and commits me to the future. For
the knowledge that I have of anyone ties me by tenuous
cords to his past and confronts me with choices for the
future. With Jesus this is even more obviously so as his
place in the past is so much greater and his hold on the
future so much more certain.

It is his death that ties us to the past and to the present. We cannot get away from his death. Death is the
one thing in life of which we who are living have no
experience. But we know Jesus' death. We know, not
merely that he died nor just how he died, but death
itself. And, in a strange but definite way, it is because
of his death that we still know him. The first disciples,
including Judas, would probably have said that they
knew Jesus fully only after he died. Paul certainly
claimed that he wanted only to "know Jesus and him
crucified." Theirs was certainly not a merely morbid attitude due to the overpowering feeling of sorrow or
guilt, for it endured. It was, rather, that they felt that
now at last they knew him for himself, in the totality of
his life, in the depth of his suffering, and in the abiding
victory of the life that he had lived. They knew him
now, not as the personification of their hopes or their
idealistic picture of the perfect man, but just as a man
who had lived his own life from beginning to end. Despite all appearances he had not been deflected from his
purpose and had not been defeated. It is in this sense
that men have been able to say that he died, as he lived,
for them—and for all men. He died for them, not as
payment of a penalty or as a substitute, but just because he was a man content to live and die without

conditions. His death is the eternal seal upon his life and the sign forever of the cost we pay for human life.

It is at times of suffering and uncertainty and of acute frustration that men, some men, come most easily to be convinced that they know Jesus. They see him facing the same suffering, uncertainty, and frustration and find strength in the mystery of his life and in the victory of his indifference to success.

The death of Jesus is in the past. We know him only as we know him now in the present and as we find him leading us into the future. This is what the resurrection means.

Knowing a person happens in life now—in my life and his life now. Knowing Jesus happens in life now—in my life and his. We know Jesus now as the key to human life and to human destiny because we know of his death and know his life in the world now.

Resurrection is in our experience. It comes to us out of the shattering things that happen as well as out of unexpected joy. It is something that happens to us as it happened to the disciples at the first Easter.

We link death and resurrection together as if they were all of a piece. But indeed they are different. The death of Jesus was public, an event that all men could know about; it happened in the past. Resurrection is personal, it is to be experienced; it points to the future.

This is not in any way to question the reality of the resurrection experiences of the first disciples, but we cannot reconstruct their experiences, any more than we would dare to imitate the circumstances of Paul's conversion. Our experience of the resurrection will be in terms of our life and our uncertainties and our suffering. But, basically, it will be the same experience—that he is as truly the way and the truth and the life as he was when he walked in Palestine, and that we are committed to his life, which is life eternal. As Ronald Gregor Smith wrote: "The decisive point here is that we in our present lives may be confronted by the reality of Christ in such a way that we may enter into a new life." [41]

Thus to know Jesus is to face the future, as it is to know anyone else. It is to face the future in all its uncertainty and risk with its inescapable choices and demands. To know him is to know that we stand at the threshold of all possible things. We realize how inadequate our response is likely to be, but knowing him we know we can be free. We see in him what freedom means. It means freedom from fear, freedom from apprehension for the consequences of our actions, freedom in personal relations, freedom to trust and to hope and to love. Jesus is the only person we know who belongs to the future. In him we welcome the future. We know him too because he is a particular man like us but, unlike us, he is truly free. He is universal man, common man, just man.

We cannot know him in isolation. We can know him only in action and in company. In knowing him we gain confidence in the belief that the mystery and the meaning of life are to be found in knowing people. In knowing him we are free to know others and even to know ourselves.

Once we have seen Jesus as man, common man, universal man, and have found in him the key to the meaning of human life, we have moved into a world of experience and thought that is limited and inarticulate unless we talk about God, for when we talk about Jesus in terms of universal, human significance we are talking in terms of God. Many years ago John MacMurray, beginning at the point at which we might end today, wrote: "The claim that Jesus of Nazareth is the incarnation of the divine personality is in fact a claim that the human personality of Jesus is universal." [42] Someone today makes the same point but puts it like this: "Go down deep enough in any human situation, wait long enough, reach far enough, and we will find its living centre to be this man standing, as Stephen saw him, at the right hand of God." [43]

If we can ever dare to talk about knowing God, we can do so only in terms of our human experience of knowing. As we have seen, we can never adequately describe or define what we mean by this mysterious but common activity by which we get to know one another. We can talk only about knowing particular persons. We can talk about knowing Jesus. We can, indeed, claim that this knowledge of Jesus has a unique, universal significance, but we can never explain this knowledge any more than we can explain human life, for it is human life. All we can say is that our knowledge of Jesus and our way of knowing him are the only keys we have to our thinking about God. The way in which we know anyone is a pointer to the meaning of life. The way we know Jesus is the pointer to what we mean by belief in God.

But the basis of all life—and the prime necessity—is to know Jesus. Some would say that is enough, though it leads to the end of the earth and beyond. Certainly it is where we must begin.

> Not only do we know God by Jesus Christ alone, but we know ourselves by Jesus Christ alone. We know life and death by Jesus Christ alone. Apart from Jesus Christ we know not what is our life, nor our death, nor God, nor ourselves.—*Blaise Pascal.*

Notes

1. John MacMurray, *The Self as Agent* (London: Faber & Faber, Ltd., 1957), p. 15. American edition: Humanities Press, 1969.

2. A. E. Taylor, *The Faith of a Moralist* (London: Macmillan and Co., Ltd., 1930, Series I), p. 89. Am. ed.: Kraus Reprint Co., 1968.

3. G. Lowes Dickenson, *J. M. E. McTaggart* (1931). Quoted in *And the Life Everlasting*, by John Baillie (London: Oxford University Press, 1934), p. 274.

4. Peter Marin, "Children of Yearning: Meditations on the Jesus Movement," *Saturday Review*, May 6, 1972.

5. See Wilhelm Herrmann, *Communion of the Christian with God* (London: Williams & Norgate, Ltd., 1913), p. 152. Am. ed.: Fortress Press, 1971.

6. John MacMurray, *Persons in Relation* (London: Faber & Faber, Ltd., 1957), p. 129. Am. ed.: Humanities Press, 1970.

7. Martin Buber, *The Knowledge of Man* (London: George Allen & Unwin, Ltd., 1965), pp. 59–71. Am. ed.: Humanities Press, 1965.

8. William James, *The Varieties of Religious Experience* (London: William Collins Sons & Co., Ltd., Fontana Books), p. 333n. Am. ed.: The Macmillan Company, 1961.

9. Helen Gardner, *Religion and Literature* (London: Faber & Faber, Ltd., 1971), p. 145. Am. ed.: Oxford University Press, Inc., 1971.

10. *Ibid.*, p. 149.

11. Owen Chadwick, *The Reformation* (The Pelican Church History series, Vol. 3, 1964), pp. 401–402. Am. ed.: Wm. B. Eerdmans Publishing Company, 1965.

12. Russel B. Nye and J. E. Morpurgo, *The Birth of the U.S.A.* (London: Penguin Books, Ltd., 1955), p. 272. Am. ed.: *History of the United States*, Vol. 1, Penguin Books, Inc., 1956.

13. *Ibid.*

14. Quotations from *Churches and the Working Classes in Victorian England*, K. S. Inglis (London: Routledge & Kegan Paul, Ltd., 1963), p. 234. Am. ed.: University of Toronto Press, 1963.

15. Albert Schweitzer, *The Quest of the Historical Jesus*, tr. into English by W. Montgomery (London: A. and C. Black, Ltd., 1922), p. 401. Am. ed.: The Macmillan Company, 1961.

16. *Ibid.*, p. 5.

17. David Cairns, *A Gospel Without Myth* (London: SCM Press, Ltd., 1960), p. 214.

18. Michael Polanyi, *Personal Knowledge: Towards a Post-Critical Philosophy* (London: Routledge & Kegan Paul, Ltd., 1958), p. 240. Am. ed.: The University of Chicago Press, 1958.

19. Sidney M. Jourard, *Disclosing Man to Himself* (D. Van Nostrand Company, Inc., 1968), p. 52.

20. MacMurray, *Persons in Relation*, p. 169.

21. Sidney M. Jourard, *To Be or Not to Be: Transparent and The Experience of Freedom*, two papers (Esalen Institute, California, 1967), p. 3.

22. Abraham Maslow, *The Farther Reaches of Human Nature* (The Viking Press, Inc., 1971), p. 270.

23. Martin Buber, *I and Thou* (London: T. and T. Clark, 1937), p. 52. Am. ed.: Charles Scribner's Sons, 1970.

24. Edwin Muir, *An Autobiography* (London: The Hogarth Press, Ltd., 1940; University Paperbacks, 1964), p. 247. Am. ed.: The Seabury Press, 1968.

25. Jourard, *Disclosing Man to Himself*, p. 173.

26. Schweitzer, *op. cit.*, p. 4.

27. Dietrich Bonhoeffer, *Letters and Papers from Prison*

(London: William Collins Sons & Co., Ltd., Fontana Books, 1959), p. 124. Am. ed.: The Macmillan Company, 1972.

28. Eberhard Bethge, *Dietrich Bonhoeffer* (London: William Collins Sons & Co., Ltd., 1970), p. 781. Am. ed.: The Macmillan Company, 1970.

29. *Ibid.*

30. Jourard, *Disclosing Man to Himself,* p. 208.

31. MacMurray, *The Self as Agent,* p. 31.

32. Sidney M. Jourard, *The Transparent Self* (D. Van Nostrand Company, Inc., 1964, 1971), p. 5.

33. Buber, *I and Thou,* p. 62.

34. Ronald Blythe, *Akenfield: Portrait of an English Village* (London: Penguin Books, Ltd., 1969, 1972), p. 199. Am. ed.: Pantheon Books, Ltd., 1969.

35. *Ibid.,* p. 17.

36. Martin Buber, *Between Man and Man,* tr. by Ronald Gregor Smith (London: Routledge & Kegan Paul, Ltd., 1947), p. 23. Am. ed.: The Macmillan Company, 1965.

37. Buber, *The Knowledge of Man,* p. 106.

38. Cairns, *op. cit.,* pp. 215–216.

39. *Ibid.,* p. 214.

40. *Ibid.,* p. 217.

41. Ronald Gregor Smith, *The Free Man* (London: William Collins Sons & Co., Ltd., 1969), p. 134. Am. ed.: *The Whole Man,* The Westminster Press, 1969.

42. B. H. Streeter (ed.), *Adventure: The Faith of Science and the Science of Faith* (London: Macmillan and Co., Ltd., 1927), p. 207.

43. Hamish Walker, from an unpublished paper.